Spiritual Blindness

MONICA NOLAN

"FOR THE GLORY OF GOD"

Copyright © 2024 by Mónica Nolan

All rights reserved. No part of this publication may be reproduced, distributed, or transmitted in any form or by any means, including photocopying, recording, or other electronic or mechanical methods, without the prior written permission of the publisher, except in the case of brief quotations embodied in critical reviews and certain other noncommercial uses permitted by copyright law.

All biblical quotations were taken from the New American Standard 1960 "NAS" Version, unless otherwise indicated.

Published by Hemingway publishers

Cover design by Hemingway publishers

ISBN: Printed in United States

Email: monica.g.nolan@gmail.com
English Edition, 2024
Printed In: United States of America

Illustrated by Joseph Nolan in the United States
joseph.k.nolan@gmail.com

Dedication

I dedicate this book to our Heavenly Father for loving me unconditionally, to the Son for redeeming my sins and giving me everlasting life, and to the Holy Spirit of God for granting me the knowledge and understanding to know him. Holy Spirit, you have been present, revealing to me what I should write. I thank You for having chosen me.

Acknowledgments

To my beloved husband, Joseph Nolan, for giving me the freedom to be able to do God's will. Thank you for your collaboration in editing and designing this book. Joe, thank you for the time and the patience that you have for me and for loving me so much. To my four children, Robert, Barbra, Victoria, and Liam; thank you for allowing me to take this time to share with others. I have taken time from being a wife and mother to be able to bless others.

It is also necessary to name my adored mother Blanca Rosa; she has passed into eternal life. I dedicate this book, Mom, to your memory! To my father, Quiterio Orlando, you were the greatest example for me as a father, friend, man, and brother in Christ Jesus. I thank our Heavenly Father for having selected the two best parents for my foundation and growth. Although I was not a great example as a daughter, you gave me the best that a daughter could ask from her parents, which is sincere and humble love.

It's of great importance to name Pastor John H. Czubkowski for his dedication as a pastor. Thank you for that ready smile that makes one feel the presence of Jesus wherever you are. Thank you for showing me the way to see things that I was not aware of, such as discipline, love, truth, and confidence.

Thank you for shepherding me for so many years and for teaching me the good way. Although the Holy Spirit moved me away from your church (building), I always carry you in my heart. Thank you!

Pastor David Greco, although I know that you do not like earthly recognition, it is necessary to express my sincere appreciation. I thank God for using you in such a way to impact my life, and I thank you for allowing yourself to be used by God. It is a privilege for me to say that you are my pastor! Thank you! Your teaching becomes more interesting each day, and the desire to learn more from God grows immensely.

Katia Sequeira, I thank God for having placed you in my path, for helping me with this task of seeing things from different perspectives, for your prayers to finish this work, and, especially, for having collaborated on this book in the Spanish version. Thank you for your time and your love!

Thanks to everyone who took the time to read this book in Spanish and make the necessary corrections: Ruth Ochomogo, Pastor Raquel Bautista de Hiraldo, Pastor Isabel Calis, Veronica Juarez, Bartolomeo Oliver, and Stella Ituarte de Perez.

Thank you, Sadie Hernandez, for your professional support, your time, and your patience in guiding me during this journey. Thank you, Haydee Pepe, for the final correction of the Spanish version. Your dedication and concern made a great difference in this book.

Thank you, Carole Montanye, for the proofreading and translation of this book from Spanish into English. Thank you for allowing God to shine through the beautiful talent that He has given you.

Thank you, Cheryl Pallaghy, for the editing, corrections, and suggestions. You have done a terrific and blessed job! Thank you for your sisterhood and your friendship. You have always been there for my family and me. Thank you for teaching me your Hebrew heritage with such passion in your heart that it is transmissible.

Thank you, Joseph Nolan, my beloved husband, for publishing this book. You have done a great job! I am so proud of you! Thank you because I know I am not an easy cookie to work with, but you persevered in every task.

God bless each one of you for your participation, strength, and time. To God be all the glory. Amen.

Prologue

The ancient Hebrew patriarchs carried a staff. Such a staff represented their authority as fathers, spiritual leaders, priests of the family, and heads of generations.

The staff was not simply the branch of a tree. The staff had symbols, marks, and names that were carved and engraved on the wood. Those symbols illustrated the names of their ancestors and the account of the events that had happened in the past. Those marks described the testimonies of those who had preceded them. The patriarchal staff was passed from generation to generation.

The staff was the instrument that was used to recall and repeat the stories, the testimonies of God's faithfulness to each family.

Moses carried the staff of God. On it, Moses had engraved his experiences with the Eternal One. On it, he recorded the ineffable name of the I AM. That was the staff that he stretched over the Red Sea.

Aaron carried the staff of the High Priest. It was the staff (rod) that, although dry, became green again (budded) as a sign of the approval of Aaron's priestly family.

David carried his staff. On it, David had inscribed his testimonies, his memories of God's faithfulness in his life. This was the staff with which he faced Goliath.

In this book, Monica raises her staff, sharing the testimony of God in her life. These are the testimonies of God in the life of a woman who, despite the sorrows of her life, persevered in faith and received healing, peace, and destiny.

The authority of Moses, Aaron, and David emanates from their staff the testimonies of God in their lives.

This publication is written with an authority that comes from the testimonies and experiences of triumph that Monica has experienced in her life. God will bless your life when you read this book.

Pastor David Greco King's Gate Church Woodland Park, New Jersey

About the Author

I was born in the city of Miramar, province of Buenos Aires, Republic of Argentina. At the age of 22, I made a big decision in my life to not only leave my family and friends but also to go to a country with different languages, customs, and traditions. For me, this was an extreme change, costing me many tears, a great deal of loneliness, and a great hunger to be loved. Something that distracted me from my loneliness was the longing to get to know new places and to work hard every day. As time went by, I got used to my new environment. I formed a new family and had two beautiful children when, suddenly, a devastating divorce visited me. I had to carry on with life, just me and two children.

I decided to go to school, and there I finished with an Associate Degree in Radio and Television. Before finishing, I got a job as a production assistant on T.V. Two years later, I met the One who was, is, and always will be the master of my heart, Jesus, while a member of the Praise Assembly Church led by Pastor John Czubkowski. Then I met the one who today is my beloved husband, Joseph, extending my family with two more children. I started working as a teacher in a Christian school and was there for three years. After twelve years had gone by, I knew that I had to finish what I had begun. It was there that I made the decision to continue my education, obtaining a Bachelor's degree in Communications with a specialization in Technology. Then, I began as a columnist, writing articles for a Christian magazine.

Fifteen years later, my family and I attended King's Gate Church, led by Pastors David and Denise Greco. Today, we are a part of New Life Christian Fellowship Church in Pennsylvania with Pastor Claude (Skip) Whitley and his wife Michelle (Shelley). I am also leading the Spanish ministry and the Youth ministry. Our growth in the Lord continues daily, and our desire to serve Him from our hearts keeps increasing.

Introduction

A very great desire took hold of my heart when I heard the Lord saying, "I want to use you for My glory." My first thought was, "Oh, Lord, being less than the smallest of all the saints, still you chose to give me the grace to write this book."

The desire of my heart is for you, when you read it, to experience the greatness of the living God and to apply to your life what God has prepared for your life from before creation and all existence.

This book has been written for all those who have gone through and are going through difficult times in their lives, for those who have been deceived by Satan's lies, for those who are of a mind to believe God above all things, for those who have no more strength, for those who want to renounce everything, for those who have been rejected, for those who want to experience the living God, the true God, the God of love. In this way, we can give all the glory to the One who is worthy of all praise, honor, and power: God our Creator. And finally, as the Apostle Paul said, "For I am convinced that neither death, nor life, nor angels, nor principalities, nor powers, nor things present, nor things to come, nor height nor depth nor anything else in all creation can separate us from the love of God which is in Christ Jesus our Lord." (Romans 8:38-39)

I have to say that I am not a theologian, but I have learned many truths throughout the Bible from people whom God placed in my path and from the investigative study I have made throughout this whole time. Quite simply, the desire of my heart is not to be better than anyone else nor to show more knowledge than anyone else but to share with you that I, too, have been deceived by the devil's lies because I used to be spiritually blind. Today, I am prepared to help you so that the same veil that was removed from my eyes through divine grace can also be removed from your eyes. When you know the forgiveness of God, His eternal love, and His unchanging truth, you will be able to see not only with your physical eyes but also with spiritual eyes. Then, you will discover the lies that Satan made you believe.

I will be sharing how to leave an emotionally destructive state and feel motivated to lead a different life, to direct yourself, to find the solution to your problems, and to trust in God, above all, for everything because that's what He did with me.

Man and woman alike, we isolate ourselves because we simply don't want to suffer. As a woman, I know that when something painful happens to us, we distance ourselves from others, provoking fights. We separate ourselves, not physically in a total way, but actually mentally. In many cases, we make ourselves disappear (putting ourselves in a box) for self-protection so that we can feel comfortable, not realizing the confinement in which we live.

Then, we settle in such a way that we don't want to leave; we simply don't want to suffer. This kind of behavior is seen in people with a spirit of mockery (sarcasm), a shouting spirit. For example, when we are in a conversation, this person speaks very loudly in order to, in one way, hide that prison inside, and he/she appears to be an authority (to know it all).

At this present time, God has placed me here to tell you something primordial (basic); it doesn't matter what you are going through in these moments or what has happened to you.

God says today that there is a solution in one form or another, there is hope, and there is a great change that is going to bless you in the most beautiful way.

On this day, God wants you to know that He will transform the ordinary life that you have lived all this time into an extraordinary one. Your experiences were badly lived experiences, and He will change them not only to give you a completely new life but also so that you may glorify Him with this completely transformed life. Everything you have gone through, He will now use for good. All your bad behaviors, He will take and change to use them in a different way so that then He will be able to use you to bless others. (Romans 8:28)

We all need God, and although many do not yet recognize it, they will sooner or later.

For now, He will use those who listen to Him and are ready to believe and trust Him. Let the Lord who changes you start from the inside. Let Him be the Lord of your heart so that He may transform you.

What was ordinary in your life will come to be extraordinary. He knows all your past situations, your present ones, and those to come. Today, God desires your attention, not to be questioned, but so that you can listen to Him and trust Him. Lamentably, we trust people so much that when they fail us, it is hard for us to trust God because we think He will do the same.

Remember: God never distances Himself from us, but it is we who distance ourselves from Him. God allowed everything past and present so that today, in the deepest way, you can hear Him saying to you: It's time to trust Me!

"Commit your way to God, trust in Him, and He will do it. He will show your righteousness as the light and your judgement as the noon day." (Psalm 37:5-6)

Blessings, Monica

Contents

Dedication III
Acknowledgments IV
Prologue VII
About The Author IX
Introduction XI

1. Blindness 1
2. Sin 9
3. Father God Vs. The Father Of All Lies 16
4. Forgiveness 20
5. Rejection 27
6. I have to choose, but i am afraid... Whom do i follow? ... 35
7. Making A Decision 41
8. Don't Delay The Process 49
9. Change Your Way Of Thinking 63
10. Jesus' sacrifice on the cross and the power of
    the blood he shed 69
11. A Real Brokenness 76
12. It's My Life And I'll Live It As I Wish 83
13. Face The Situations 91
14. Let Us Not Become Stagnant 98
15. Like Trees 106
16. Trust Him 113
17. The Power Of God While We Wait 123
18. Dominion Over Everything 130

19. References 136

Chapter 1
Blindness

 I was completely blind. I saw no other way except my way, and when I was tired of fighting with my own strength, it was then that I recognized that I couldn't do it anymore. I shouted to heaven and asked God's forgiveness for not having listened before. In Proverbs 28:13 it says, "He who conceals his sins will not prosper; but he who confesses and forsakes them will find mercy."

There are times when, because of the situations we are going through, it is difficult to trust in God, especially because we do not see Him. How can anyone believe in something or someone unseen? Sometimes, it may be difficult, but not impossible. Air and wind are not visible, but they exist; otherwise, we would not be able to breathe. When the disciples told Thomas after the resurrection that Jesus had come to visit them, Thomas said to them, "Unless I see the nail prints in his hands and put my finger into the place of the nails, and put my hand into His side, I will not believe." (John 20:25)

Thomas was very specific regarding his requirement for believing. He explained clearly that for him to be able to believe, it was necessary to see with his own eyes, to touch with his own hands what the others had seen. How many times have we said the same thing, "unless I see it, I won't believe it," and we fall into that famous saying, "seeing is believing." In a certain way, if we examine this event, it wasn't hard for the disciples to believe because they saw Him with their own eyes. (Perhaps, although for just an instant, they too could have doubted!) How many times did you think that Jesus was visiting you, but at the same time, you didn't believe? And that instant of doubt came to your mind, and you said, "No, it can't be, it's just my imagination!" We want to trust God, but at the same time, we think it's impossible to do it.

I think that Thomas' skepticism made him suffer after the crucifixion, but he had even more pain, having regretted not being present at that moment. You will ask me why I think so, and I will tell you it is because his own blindness led him not to be there. Have you ever said, "If I had been there, this would never have happened," or "if I had gone, everything would be

1. Blindness

different." Thomas regretted considerably not having been there at that precise moment and at the exact hour because there is always a moment of regret that makes you reflect. Then, when Jesus arose from the dead, Thomas wasn't there either, and he could not accept the fact that Jesus had indeed arisen; he believed that the body of Jesus had been stolen from the tomb. His blindness did not allow him to see, and because of it, he did not believe.

Perhaps you are going through something similar to Thomas. They have spoken to you about God, His Son Jesus, that there is hope and thousands of other things that you should be able to see with spiritual eyes, but you never believed. You never gave yourself a chance to believe first in order to see later. At this time, I think that doubts, questions, and other things are coming to your mind.

I ask you now to try to see this situation as when you lose someone, and you are looking for them. I imagine Thomas with a feeling of desperation, doing the impossible to find the body of Jesus. Suddenly, he begins to walk everywhere. He goes through terrible moments confronting the religious and civil leaders. Maybe he even crosses the desert and, already losing hope and exhausted, returns. Poor Thomas! Tired, he goes back to where the rest of the disciples are, but before entering, he feels ashamed, not for having to confront them (since he would have calmly told them that he was searching for the Master's body), but because he realized that he had lost hope. Being so focused on doing things by his own efforts, he lost the chance that the others had simply because they trusted and knew how to wait on God.

Spritual Blindness

When the disciples were finally united, Thomas confessed to them that he had used all his strength and all his being on his own search, on his own way of seeing things. Shut up in his own vision, and he got tired. He confessed how he felt because he had never been there at the precise place and the exact hour. Thomas was so focused on himself that he even became selfish because he only thought about himself, to the point that the state of blindness was keeping him from seeing. So it is with us through the decisions we make in life. We can also lose good opportunities to enjoy precious encounters with Jesus.

I remember when I was 11 years old, my best friend wanted to share with me the church where she and her family used to go. When we got to the place, I reacted in a confused manner. In my belief and knowledge, the only church that existed was the Catholic church in the city, which my parents and I used to attend on a few occasions; maybe you could say once a year or once every two years. Jesus is constantly calling us, but unfortunately, we are spiritually deaf and blind, and we are not able to answer His call. Everything works for good, and at that time, I didn't listen because I didn't believe and I didn't see, but God allowed everything that happened in my life so that I could speak to you today and tell you that God does exist. God is love. God always was, always is, and always will be at your side. If you accept Jesus as Savior in your heart, and you repent of your sins, He will forgive you, and you will have eternal life. Say "Goodbye" to your problems, to what holds you in bondage, spiritual blindness, because Jesus loves you and is waiting for you to accept Him so that He can bless you and set you free.

1. Blindness

Thomas searched desperately; his same desperation did not let him see any farther. Who looks for something or someone when he already has it? Why did Thomas look for Jesus? After Jesus had chosen his disciples, He walked with them for three years, He taught them many truths, and He performed many miracles in which they participated: He healed the sick, He gave sight to the blind, he made the lame walk, he raised many from the dead ... Thomas listened to Jesus himself saying that it was necessary for Him to go to the Father so that the Holy Spirit could descend so that there would be no orphans or abandonment on the earth. Thomas was aware of the crucifixion of Jesus, but he doubted that Jesus would be resurrected on the third day. Thomas' blindness had to have increased the doubt in him, the doubt that caused unbelief and insecurity and not being able to see farther. Blindness in a person brings doubts, and those doubts produce unbelief. Thomas had accepted Jesus when he decided to follow Him, and he knew that Jesus would rise from the dead afterward and that they would receive the Holy Spirit. Unfortunately, Thomas was concentrating on what he did not see. For him, if he didn't see it, he wouldn't be able to be certain.

Having to see in order to believe is a very big problem that exists in the human being. We are not trained to trust in anything that we do not see. On this day, perhaps you may not see Jesus, but you should be able to feel Him if you let Him because He is right there where you are. He wants you to open your heart so that you can receive Him, and He can lead you on the good path. You only have to believe in order to see, and in that way, you can have a loving relationship with Jesus. When you surrender your heart, He will transform your mind, the blindness will fall, and you will see.

Sooner or later, we are going to have to do God's will. He will not stop calling us until we come to Him. Jesus did it, does it, and will do it "with cords of eternal love" until He has us with Him. You and I are His creation. God's word says that every knee shall bow and every tongue confess that He is King ... "So that in the name of Jesus every knee of those in heaven and on earth, and under the earth shall bow; and every tongue confess that Jesus Christ is Lord for the glory of God the Father." (Philippians 2: 10-11)

Don't think about it anymore. Release everything that ties you to the world. Surrender yourself fully to the King. It is written, "Delight yourself in the Lord, and he will give you the desires of your heart. Commit your way unto the Lord; trust in Him; and He will do it. He will bring forth your righteousness as the light and your judgment as the noonday." (Psalm 37: 4-6)

I must confess that it took me a while to understand this verse since I thought that if I delighted in God, he would give me everything that I wanted (does this sound familiar?) Always thinking about ME, Me, Me, and about what I wanted. Let us analyze this verse together. What does He want to teach us? Why does it say, "Delight yourself in the Lord"? Let us look at the word in "Vine's Dictionary." The meaning of this word "delight" is the Hebrew verb "sunedomai" or "to rejoice with," or "to delight oneself in, together with." To delight yourself with the very one inside in one thing. How do we delight in God? By reading the Bible and going to church to hear his message. Why is it necessary to do all this? Because when He lives

1. Blindness

inside us, it is then our responsibility to know what God wants from us. Now, I delight myself in Him so that I can understand what it is that He wants. The plan and purpose are God's and only He knows them because when we apply all these principles to our minds, we will come to know what is God's desire for us. He will grant the desires of our hearts because they are, at the same time God's desires, because now He lives in us for His purpose and plan.

If at this moment, the desire of your heart is to be able to be free, let the Lord remove the blindness that is in your spiritual eyes keeping you from seeing. He will make you truly free from everything afflicting you: from stress, from depression, from doubt, from sorrow, from sickness, from blindness, free to live joyfully, peacefully, quietly, confidently, and securely. The only thing you have to do is to ask God in the name of Jesus.

There was a man of the Pharisees called Nicodemus, a ruler among the Jews. This man came to Jesus at night and said to Him, "Rabbi, we know that You have come from God as a teacher, for no one can do these signs that You do unless God is with him." Jesus answered and said, "Truly, truly I say to you that he who is not born again cannot see the kingdom of God." Nicodemus said to Him, "How can a man be born when he is old? Can he, perhaps, enter his mother's womb a second time and be born?" It was hard for Nicodemus to believe what Jesus was telling him because he had spiritual blindness, he saw everything in the physical, and so he asked Jesus how an old man, already born, could again enter his mother's womb. Jesus answered, "Truly, truly I say to you that what is not born of water and of the Spirit cannot enter the kingdom of God.

That which is born of the flesh is flesh; and that which is born of the Spirit is spirit. Do not marvel that I said to you, "Ye must be born again. The wind blows where it wishes, and you hear its sound, but you neither know from where it is coming nor where it is going; so is everything that is born of the Spirit." Nicodemus answered and said, "How can this be so?" Jesus answered and said, "Are the teachers of Israel, and don't you know this? Truly, truly, I say to you that what we know, we speak and we testify of what we have seen; and you do not accept our testimony. If I told you earthly things and you do not believe, how can you believe if I tell you heavenly things? No one has descended from heaven except he who had ascended to heaven: the Son of Man who is in heaven. And as Moses lifted up the serpent in the desert, so it is necessary that the Son of Man be lifted up so that everyone who believes in Him, should not perish, but have eternal life."(John 3:1-15)

"For God so loved the world that He gave His only begotten Son so that whoever believes in Him shall not perish, but have eternal life. For God did not send His Son into the world to condemn the world but so that all the world might be saved through Him." (John 3: 16-17)

Chapter 2
Sin

The first book of the Bible, Genesis, tells us that from the beginning, God saw that the earth was formless and empty. Then, as soon as He set it in order, he formed man, breathed in the spirit of life, and placed him in the Garden of Eden. From the man's rib, He formed a woman. God gave them instructions to follow, but only one commandment with a consequence. "But of the tree of the knowledge of good and evil you are not to eat; for in the day that you eat of it you will surely die." (Genesis 2:17)

Sin is not recent. To reach a greater understanding regarding the origin of sin, we first must understand the reason and the cause that it entered the world. Sin is the manifestation of rebellion. Being rebellious makes us opposed to something or someone. According to Vine's Dictionary, the word "rebellious" in Greek is "apeithes". Disobedient in Greek is 'apeitheo," and it means "to reject, to be persuaded, to reject a belief, to be disobedient." Exactly when did sin begin? The answer is in heaven when Lucifer disobeyed the plans of God. Then, when Lucifer was thrown from the Third Heaven (remember that God is Holy and perfect and therefore sin separates us completely from God), he left His presence, being hurled to the second heaven. "Lucifer" means "morning light". When he fell, he turned into Satan, which means "adversary." (W.E. Vine, 1984) Satan is the adversary of God and of His creation.

If we don't follow God, we are following Satan. With this horrendous reality in mind, the obvious question is: Why did God create Satan? No, God created Lucifer, but he disobeyed and sinned, and for this reason, he was thrown from the Third Heaven. On the way to the second heaven, he was developing all the characteristics that degraded him into Satan, the adversary of God. When Lucifer fell, he also took with him one-third of the angels in heaven who were also in rebellion against God. In the process, Satan established his government consisting of principalities, powers, governors, armies, and demons whose work it is to convince us that sinning is something common and natural and that the consequences aren't all that bad. He lies to you, saying that doing good is not good because it isn't the trend and that doing bad is the right way. That is when the disaster begins.

Now, we must confront hardships, problems, and opposing circumstances in our lives. We become vulnerable and that provokes us to rebellion. For example, if we observe children older than thirteen, we can clearly see how demons come to play with their minds. These demons convince these children that nobody wants or loves them. They may try to convince other children that they are worthless because of their appearance. They convince others by saying that they can do everything without anyone's help. They become independent not only from those they love but also their friends, their parents, and they even become independent from their Creator. Unfortunately, they die spiritually.

God created Adam. The Bible says, "He formed man from the dust of the earth and breathed into his nostrils the breath of life, and man became a living soul." (Genesis 2:7) When Adam and Eve sinned against God, they were destitute and separated from God's presence, beginning a life independent from their Creator.

We are now born with that Adamic, sinful, seared, and rebellious spirit that makes us act for ourselves, thinking that we are doing things the right way when, in the eyes of God, we are not. We give place to our soul to take complete control. Now, our desires are for what we want, and we are deceived by our adversary, who then becomes our god. A spiritual blindness enters us, and a spiritual deafness that hears only the voice of Satan and his demons.

This blindness is so great in humanity that when we hear Satan's voice, we think we are hearing the voice of God. Our carnal eyes see that things are going well for us, whether financially or in our personal lives, and we fill ourselves more and more with material possessions. We are happy about it because we keep believing that we are being blessed by God. When we fall into divorce, depression, adultery, and thousands of other things, some of us become angry with God and blame Him for allowing these things to happen when, on the other hand, God has been calling us from the time we were in our mothers' womb. We never hear God's voice, but the voice of Satan instead.

Satan talks us into doing what is bad or keeps us from doing what is good and acceptable. He convinces us that we can do things that are not good without consequences. Then, he reverses everything so that we fall into his scheme of things and then he can condemn us, and he does condemn us in this horrible condition, so we no longer know which way to run. Then we think, "Why try to do anything?" Nothing matters to us because confusion enters our minds, and we don't know what to do. We don't care about our physical condition or how we dress because we no longer like ourselves. It is no longer our nature. Because we were created by God to do good, and what Satan offers us is something filthy, false, and diabolical that does not match our principles. It shocks us, but already convinced, we keep following that awful, sinful road to perdition.

Girls and boys behave insolently. The devil makes them think that with physical beauty, they can manipulate any situation and any people. They use their bodies seductively as a tool for their whims and physical necessities. God says that the intimate physical relationship is only for marriage; the deceiver comes and tells them, "Well then, if you have to be married to satisfy your body, then masturbate; that way, you won't have any contact with anyone." Let me tell you something: those who say these things are the demons themselves who want to satisfy themselves with your body, because they live off you, and they convince you that it is something natural because, by doing these things, they nourish themselves. That's why when you maintain relationships, you do it (have sexual intercourse) with your first boyfriend or girlfriend, then you have a fight, and comes another and another until this is transformed into a daily habitual necessity that, without knowing it, you are making a "covenant" with everyone with whom you carry on sexual, physical relationships. Masturbation will lead you to early sexual relationships that are illicit (fornication and adultery). Such practices have consequences like abortions (murder and death) and it leads to disillusions, mental and sentimental unhappiness, cutting your skin, self-hatred, bitterness, and suicide.

Satan steals our identity from us when he takes authority over our lives to the point that some no longer know if they are men or women. They begin to date homosexuals and heterosexuals, transgenders. They experiment with drugs and alcohol to conceal the pain, and when they run out of money, they steal, and some resort to prostitution. And Satan lies to them, telling them that homosexuals and transgenders are human beings who fall in love with other human beings of the same sex because they are already born that way. How by any means is this "love" (according to what they believe) which tricks them into changing their genders and destroying their lives? This is "pure sin."

Did you know that God said male and female? The question is, why Man and Woman? The answer is so they can procreate. Man and man or woman and woman cannot procreate. Then the devil deceives them, saying if the man mistreats you, you can look for a woman who will understand you, and the same with a man; he can look for a man because he knows what you have gone through, and he deceives them. We are experiencing the era of same-sex marriage, bringing confusion to new generations. Since they cannot procreate, they adopt, thinking that they are doing good work, but the only thing they are doing is bringing confusion to those innocent children who, when they go to school, can't celebrate Father's Day and Mother's day because they have in their house the same sex. Satan came to steal, kill, and destroy; "The thief only comes to steal, kill, and destroy; I have come so that you may have life and so that you may have it abundantly. (John 10:10) The enemy hates us because he knows that God loves us unconditionally; that is why the devil is always trying to convince you to fall into sin to separate you from your Creator and thus, destroy you.

The druggie no longer has control of himself, and he starts committing atrocities, committing orgies. This segment of the population in the world that we know as teenagers are the favorites of satanic work because Satan has stolen his identity, and they can't tell for sure what is yes and what is no.

1 Corinthians 6:9 says, "Do you not know that the unrighteous will not inherit the kingdom of God? Do not be deceived; neither fornicators, nor idolaters, nor adulterers, nor effemi-

nate, or homosexuals, nor thieves, nor the covetous, nor drunkards, nor revilers, nor swindlers will inherit the kingdom of God."

In Galatians 5:16-17 it says, "But I say walk in the Spirit and do not satisfy the desires of the flesh, because the desire of the flesh sets its desire against the Spirit and the Spirit against the flesh; for these are in opposition to each other, so that you many not do the things that you please."

Die to sin, and you will live. "Because the law of the Spirit of life in Christ Jesus has freed me from the law of sin and death." (Romans 8:2)

"And if the Spirit of Him who raised Jesus from the dead dwells in you, He who raised Christ Jesus from the dead will also give life to your mortal bodies through his Spirit who dwells in you." (Romans 8:11).

"Do you not know that when you present yourselves to someone as slaves for obedience, you are slaves to the one whom you obey, either of sin resulting in death or of obedience, resulting in righteousness?" (Romans 6:16)

"I am speaking in human terms because of the weakness of your flesh. For just as you presented your members as slaves to impurity and to lawlessness, so now present our members as slaves to righteousness, resulting in sanctification." (Romans 6:19)

Chapter 3
Father God Vs. The Father Of All Lies

The Kingdom of God was instituted by the Father, the Son, and the Holy Spirit, which is ruled by the only one God, the Creator of all existence. The nature of the Kingdom of God is everything that is good. Satan's kingdom is everything that is evil because his character is wicked. Satan's kingdom is comprised of Satan, principalities, powers, rulers of darkness, and demons.

3. Father god vs. The father of all lies

God's kingdom is totally opposed to everything, which refers to the father of all lies, known as Satan. Everything that is of God's kingdom is not related to the liar. For this reason, they are in constant warfare, and with us as their objective, we participate in it daily. Father God desires the best for us, while the father of all lies seeks to destroy us, pretending he wants what is best for you until he wins you over. Once he wins your mind, he destroys you little by little until he kills you.

We must acquire discernment to be able to be more than conquerors. Then we will understand that in this world, we will have afflictions, but Jesus has overcome the world. When we know that He who is in us is greater than he who is in the world and that if we follow God and obey Him, He will give us the strength to face any situation because it is written, "I can do all things in Christ who strengthens me. " (Philippians 4:13)

Both God and Satan have specific natures. God's nature is "love, joy, peace, patience, kindness, goodness, faith, gentleness, and self-control." (Galatians 5:22-23) God's nature is righteousness, purity, wisdom, justice, honesty, a clean heart, sincerity, knowledge, understanding, grace, mercy, excellence, forgiveness, compassion, and devotion.

Satan's nature is "hatred, murder, violence, ruthlessness, resentment, rejection, fear, jealousy, envy, lying." (Galatians 5:19-21) Satan brings condemnation, shame, pride, blame, lust, greed, covetousness, vengeance, retaliation, slander, a critical spirit, terror, lack of forgiveness, no mercy, no pity, murmurings, selfishness, and gossip. Satan controls principalities and powers and these possess his roots. These roots can be identified as unbelief, concealment, fear, rejection, jealousy and envy, and anger with oneself or with others. When we give Satan authority and these roots take hold of us, his kingdom attributes manifest in us, and we act accordingly. We think according to our desires, and we say things that we are sorry for afterward.

Many times, I have read this passage in the Bible that speaks about the power of the tongue. Proverbs 18:21 says, "Life and death are in the power of the tongue and he who loves it will eat of its fruits." We say many things that wound others without thinking of the consequences. Our way of speaking identifies us with the nature of our adversary because, from what abounds in the heart, the mouth speaks. "The good man, out of the good treasure of his heart, brings forth what is good; and the evil man, out of the evil treasure of his heart, brings forth evil; for his mouth speaks from that which fills his heart." (Luke 6:45)

We fail to recognize the power that our words have when we speak, not knowing that we can give life as well as death. When we speak, God listens, and Satan does too. They hear everything that we say, and they fulfill what we proclaim. If we call people asses, idiots, ignorant, etc., or if they have called us things like this, we must cancel these words. We must do this in order for us to be free from that filthy kingdom that makes us think we are worthless and that we don't amount to anything. God tells us that we were made in his image and resemble Him, and we are capable of anything.

Those voices that you hear are telling you things like, "You are a good-for-nothing," "You are an old man or woman," "You won't be able to have any children because you and your spouse are advanced in age," etc. God's word tells the story of Sarah and Abraham. "God visited Sarah, as He had said, and

3. Father god vs. The father of all lies

he did with Sarah what He had spoken. And Sarah conceived and gave Abraham a son in her old age in the time that God had told her." (Genesis 21:1) Sarah was advanced in age, but we keep believing Satan's lies when we say, "But that happened long ago; we're living in different times now." We believe Satan's lies because, yes, the times are different, but God is the same yesterday, today, and always. (Hebrews 13:8)

In the book of Galatians, Paul talks about "The works of the flesh and the fruit of the Spirit." The work of the flesh refers to the desires in our mind, what we want, and what makes us feel good. Our minds can be nourished by God or polluted by Satan. But if our minds are polluted by Satan, our desires will be evil. Perhaps those desires want to make us feel good, but in the end, they will result in an evil outcome.

Now that we know and have a greater understanding concerning these two spiritual natures, it would be good to examine ourselves with respect to our daily actions. Let us analyze ourselves to see if we find any attitudes, emotions, or thoughts that pertain to the dark kingdom that might control us. Examine yourself daily to see under which one of those two kingdoms do you dwell and whom do you obey.

Chapter 4
Forgiveness

    A while back, my family and I went to the country of my birth to give my testimony. I wanted to share the wonders that God had done in my life and in my family, how He had saved our souls, and all the changes He had done for our good. But a week before going to the church, I felt the need to speak to the pastor because I felt like there was something wrong inside me. The verse in the Bible, "Be imitators of me just as I am of

Christ." (1 Corinthians 11:1) came to me. This means to walk like He walked and to speak like He spoke. I realized that I was far from all that. Although I loved and obeyed God, my walk wasn't always like Jesus'. I couldn't imagine that Jesus had said some of the things I said. My talk, walk, and behavior were not coming from Jesus. Then where was my character coming from? Why was I acting in a certain way? Why did I want to but could not imitate Jesus? What was it that was interfering inside of me? Obviously, something was acting contrary to the way Jesus acted.

My Christian walk was like a roller coaster. One day, I would be fine, happy, content, feeling as though I could touch heaven with my hands. The next day, I would feel depressed, have no desire to work, I wouldn't laugh and if I did, it would be to cover my sadness inside. I would scream instead of talk. I was living in a constant struggle. I could not concentrate on what I had to do, and it was robbing me of my peace.

This emotional imbalance was giving me insecurity to the extent that I couldn't do any planning. I went to the pastor's house and shared with them how I was feeling, and we began praying. The Holy Spirit, through the pastor, said that· I had to forgive my mother and that I had to ask for forgiveness. When our meeting ended, we said good-bye, and I went to my mother's house, meditating on the way about everything the Holy Spirit had spoken that afternoon.

There were many questions that passed through my mind at that moment about the relationship that I had with my mother from my childhood. Our relationship was not ugly. What I did remember was that I always wanted to be with her. I liked school, I had friends there, but I preferred to stay with my mother because she treated me well and gave me everything I liked. If my sisters and I misbehaved, she would punish them, but she never punished me. When the Holy Spirit told me to forgive my mother, I looked at heaven and said, "What do I have to forgive my mother for, God; please tell me what?" The fact that I had to forgive her confused me. Although I was very sure and had decided to do what the Lord had told me to do, I kept asking myself, "For what do I have to forgive my mother or ask forgiveness for?"

The decision to forgive my mother was in my heart, but I felt that something was holding me back. I really wanted to be free of that, but even then, it was not easy to do. First, because I thought I would offend her if I told her I forgave her. Second, I couldn't think of anything bad that had happened between us. I understand that human beings block things from their minds that hurt them so they won't suffer. With the passage of time, that remains a safeguard so that eventually, they don't remember a thing. Life continues, and we have to survive. We can't concentrate on the past but rather move forward and bury the pain and suffering.

At that time, I couldn't remember anything at all that I had to forgive my mother for, but even so, it was necessary for me to believe and obey God because he told me to do it. I. had to obey Him. I realized that it wasn't for me to understand; it was for me to obey. At this point, it was no longer important to remember the "what" or the "why," I was to forgive my mother and ask her for forgiveness because the lack of forgiveness was limiting her blessings and mine.

More than anything, I wanted my mother to be free forever so that she could experience a personal relationship with Jesus.

4. Forgiveness

I wanted to be free of everything that was binding me to everything that was taking the joy out of my life. And the only thing that could free both of us was for us to ask God for forgiveness, to forgive ourselves, and to forgive each other.

Once I had made that decision, I approached my mother to tell her that we had to talk, but I couldn't say anything to her. I asked myself, "Why can't I tell her that I need to talk to her? What is holding me back?" I told my husband, "I can't ask my mother for forgiveness, and I want to do it, but something is keeping me from doing it." He suggested that we pray, and when we finished praying, I felt at peace. I approached her again. I tried again, but my mouth remained closed, and I could not speak. I called my husband and we prayed again. I tried again for the third time. For two days, my husband and I kept praying to break whatever it was that was holding me back. I remember that I kept repeating, "I can do all things through Christ who strengthens me," several times. The third and final time, when I went to my mother and said, "Mom, we have to talk," she said, "Is everything alright?" I told her, "We need to go to a private place to talk." My husband stayed in the living room with our little daughter, and we went into the bedroom. It wasn't easy for me to confront my mother to ask her forgiveness, but with the help of the Holy Spirit, I succeeded.

Satan finds out everything that is happening, and he anticipates what we will do. When we want to do God's will and obey Him, Satan wants to keep us from doing it. But when we make the decision, God is already fighting for us. "Little children, you are of God, you have overcome them; because greater is he that is in you than he that is in the world" (1 John 4:4). We also know that we can do everything through our all-powerful God (Philippians 4:13). "Then what shall we say to this? If God is for us, who can stand against us?" (Romans 8:31).

Satan does not want us to be happy or to have healthy relationships with others. He is an opponent; he fights, he hates us, and thus, he wants us to be with the rest of his dominion. He knows that by NOT forgiving others or ourselves, we are opening a door to Satan, and by doing so he can do with us whatever he wants. "Be kind and compassionate to one another, forgiving each other, just as in Christ God forgave you." (Ephesians 4:32)

When we obey God by asking His forgiveness and forgiving the offenses of others so that God will forgive us, Satan gets so enraged that he even does the impossible to make us disobey. The first and second times I attempted to talk to my mother were devastating. Although I had prayed with the pastors and then with my husband, when I went to talk to my mother, I could say nothing. The third time I tried, I finally was able to speak; when I spoke, the chain of unforgiveness was broken.

I asked her forgiveness, I forgave her, and it was like a wall that had fallen. We ended up in the bedroom, hugging, crying, and repentant. Seeing through my tears, I found myself sitting in her lap like a baby. There was a constant flow of forgiveness, and we couldn't stop forgiving each other and repeating the words I love you. I can say that it was a beautiful moment because I had never kissed my mother so many times nor has she kissed me like that. From that glorious moment on, our relationship had been reinforced with complete respect and honor. I remember that I couldn't stop caressing my mother. I kept touching her hands, kissing them in gratitude for everything she had done for me in my life.

For the first time, I succeeded in showing my mother the love that I had always felt for her. I understood that, on account of the unforgiveness, I could never make that great love come to light in us. Unforgiveness blinds you so that you can never see the beauty that surrounds you. For the first time, I could see the beauty, the tenderness, and the sweetness that my mother possessed. I thank God for everything He has done, everything He does, and everything He will do in my life. How grateful I am to Him for having freed us forever.

Forgiveness freed us. In the Bible, Exodus 20:12 says, "Honor your father and your mother that your days may be long upon the earth which the Lord your God has given you." Lack of forgiveness kept me from honoring my mother, but when I forgave her and asked her forgiveness, honoring her was no longer a forced thing but something natural because forgiveness removes every obstacle. If you have not forgiven your father or your mother, do it and you will see how your life changes forever.

We returned to the United States, where my family and I reside. Six months later, my mother accepted Jesus as her Lord and Savior. A little while later, my father accepted Jesus as well. Their souls were saved. Forgiveness is a key that leads to freedom. Forgiving others of their offenses is of utmost importance because God says that if we don't forgive, He will not forgive us. "And forgive us our debts, as we have also forgiven our debtors." (Matthew 6:12) Ask God for forgiveness, forgive yourself, and forgive others.

In time, I learned that the lack of forgiveness holds back blessings in our lives, and although my parents' souls were saved, it took a lot of work to do it. Afterward, they started their freedom by forgiving their debtors, forgiving themselves, and asking God for forgiveness. They began to attend the church in the city where they were living, and they learned many things about God. My relationship with my parents became beautiful. Whenever we talked on the phone, we read the Bible together and prayed. Now, they are resting in peace with their Redeemer.

Chapter 5
Rejection

Rejection is one of the most devastating feelings of a human being. When someone has been rejected, not only does he or she feel the rejection, but they will also reject others. Whether they are rejected by a friend, a father, a mother, a relative, or a coworker, it makes them lose confidence in others and themselves. This can cause confusion, insecurity, and loss of identity. It is hard for them to concentrate on what they are doing

Spritual Blindness

and causes disorganization. When people tell them that they are great workers, they cannot believe it simply because they are never satisfied or convinced about what they are doing. They look for perfection in everything they do so they won't be criticized by others. They work super hard to satisfy others; in other words, they become people pleasers.

Rejected people don't believe they can be loved. They think no one could possibly love them. Their feelings of rejection cause them to reject others instead. This is an active and constant contention in people who have been rejected. Human beings were created good and with God's love. Though they may have wandered from God or may have never known Him, that is to say, they never had a personal experience or relationship with Him. They suffer because the spirit of rejection has caused a root of bitterness to grow, which makes them hardened, acidic, and noxious. This bitterness will also cause jealousy and envy towards others.

In many cases, but not always, one could say that the spirit of rejection begins in the mother's womb. In my case, according to my parents' plans, I was supposed to be a boy. Obviously, God's plans were different because, according to Jeremiah 1:5 "Before you were formed in the womb, I knew you." God already knew my gender.

My parents' wish was for me to be born a boy. This opened a door for the enemy, causing the spirit of rejection to enter me. This spirit operated in me for years, manipulating situations in my life, taking away my identity, and bringing me confusion. While my girlfriends were fixing their hair or painting their nails, I was playing soccer with the boys. They were playing with dolls and having tea parties, and I was climbing trees and building forts with the boys. I had played basketball for eleven years, and when I practiced with the boys, I felt more comfortable because I identified more with them. My mind was confused because I was born as a girl, but since my parents' desire from the time I was in my mother's womb was for me to be a boy, it opened a door for Satan so that the spirit of rejection could enter in me. They were so sure I would be a boy that they never even picked out a girl's name for me.

When I minister to people for freedom and healing, I always carry paper and a pencil with me to take notes. The first question I ask is if they were wanted or not when they were conceived? I asked them what their parents wanted to have, a boy or a girl? If their parents were married before they were conceived? ...and many other questions. Then, I draw a tree with a trunk and roots. The tree has a shapely top with a firm, robust trunk, and strong, long roots. I explain to them that although this tree looks healthy, it may be that its roots are not. If the soil where the tree was planted is contaminated, the tree will also be contaminated; it will not bear fruit. Even if it does, the fruit will also be contaminated. I then write on the trunk the word "rejection."

Years ago, my husband had to cut down a pear tree in our backyard. The tree didn't look sick; it was tall and large, but when it bore fruit, they were decayed (bad and rotten). It grieved us to cut it down, but, in reality, it was of no use to us except to accumulate flies, ants, and many bees.

In time, we realized that the former owners of this house, before planting the pear tree, had thrown out and buried a lot of garbage like glass, plastic, motor oil, tennis balls, car parts, and many other things that had contaminated the soil in the ground.

The garbage was buried deep down and couldn't be seen. When the pear tree was cut down, you could see everything that was there. The roots of the tree kept growing and began to expand, receiving contaminated food that affected the tree and its fruit to the point of almost killing it. It's the same way with us. It's important to know what we have received, what our nourishment was, if our parents wanted us, what sex they wanted, if we were despised or not loved, etc.

People who have been rejected automatically receive negative nourishment, causing bitterness to develop in their roots. Bitterness is a stronghold of Satan and has roots of disbelief, jealousy, envy, rejection, fear, and the occult, and can even drive them to death.

I am not comparing a human being to a tree; this is simply an analogy to show that in the spiritual realm, demons have roots. These roots of bitterness, jealousy, and envy end in death, and although the person may not end up killing themselves, but in their heart, they will have the desire to be dead or lack the will to live.

I never understood why death always pursued me. In my mind, I always wanted to die. I was too scared to kill myself, but yes, many times, I wanted and desired to be dead. It is very important to bring to light these spirits to remove Satan's authority, to forgive others, and to forgive ourselves. When I discovered that I had been rejected by my parents while in my mother's womb and started canceling the rejection spirit in me, doors of blessing began to open in my life, helping me each day to be more and more free. This spiritual freedom allowed me to be able to listen to God's Holy Spirit clearly.

I remember one day in a church, someone was praying for me, and I heard him ask God to bring my mother's womb to my memory to reveal what had happened when she was pregnant with me. I began to pray, and I asked the Holy Spirit to show me the truth. He brought to my mind things that I had not remembered.

One day, it came to my memory that I went to visit my father at his job. We were talking when a friend of his came by. My father introduced his friend to me, and he commented that I was very pretty. My father told him with a smile on his face, "Very pretty, but she was supposed to be a boy." My parents already had two girls, and they wanted a boy. It was very important to have a male child to continue the family name since the female children would marry and continue their husband's family name.

Those wishes and confessions that my mother made while I was in her womb and my parent's lack of knowledge of spiritual things opened a door for Satan to take authority over my life and to deposit in me the spirit of rejection. This spirit of rejection began to show itself in my life from the time I was born to the extent that as I matured, they matured, too. Roots of bitterness, envy, and jealousy began to grow in me. As I grew, these spirits manifested themselves in me in a horrendous way. I did things I didn't want to do because they went against my will. I did them without understanding the reason why.

Getting back to my father's conversation with his friend, he told him as a "joke," saying that, "Yes, very pretty, but she was supposed to be a boy," only because they wanted a boy. I paid close attention to the conversation as my father told him the story of when my mother was in the hospital ready to have me and... I was born.

She called my father at work, and when my father asked her," Is it a boy?" my mother told him, "No, it's another flip-flop!" Satan was having a great party. I not only passed from being a "joke" to a "flip-flop," but last of all, I didn't even have a "name."

My father asked her," What name shall we give her?" "I have no idea," my mother said.

My father's job was at the theater in the city. When I was born, it was showing the movie "Looking for Monica." My father saw that name on the marquee and said," Monica, her name will be Monica!" The priest came to register me and asked my mother if she had a name for me, and she said, "Her name will be Monica Ruth." She had always liked the name Ruth with the "th" at the end.

The priest said, "I'm sorry, but the Catholic Church does not allow Jewish names, and Ruth is a Jewish name."

Without giving it much thought, my mother said to him, "Then she will be called Monica Graciela." Incidentally, Graciela comes from the word grace. God's grace is what has saved me!

Finally, I began to understand my temperament, my behavior regarding doing what I didn't want to do, how I treated others, and a heap of attitudes opposed to my will.

God has given us a spirit of power and self-control, and when I did things outside of my will, I would feel that something in me was not right, that something had to change, and, thanks to the Holy Spirit, this was revealed in me. I forgave my parents and asked God, too, to forgive them. I removed Satan's authority from myself that had taken my life through that sin, and I ordered the spirit of rejection to leave my life in the name of Jesus.

At this moment, your mind is receiving memories, things that perhaps you have buried in the deepest part of your being so that they wouldn't hurt you, but now is the time for you to dig them up. Do not let Satan keep mistreating you as he has been doing all this time.

Perhaps in the past, you were hurt, and you don't want to remember. It hurts you to think about it, and you don't want that pain, but Jesus can remove, erase, and heal what is in you if you believe and if you ask Him.

I encourage you to trust God, who does not reject nor disappoint, nor hurt us, nor abandon us, nor forsake us. He will heal your pain from the inside now, and it will never hurt you again.

I remember one day when I cut my finger, I washed the cut and covered it with a bandage. Night came, and I forgot to take it off and went to sleep. The next day, the pain woke me up, and when I took off the bandage, I found my finger infected, inflamed, and very painful. The bandage had covered my cut, but it had not healed it; in fact, it had infected my finger. That's how it is with us when we cover our wounds and our pains that we have received with the passing of time, but they are not healed, and they keep on infecting us inside little by little.

The spirit of rejection and bitterness had infected me in such a way that from a very young age, my desire to avenge myself (get even with) against someone who had raped me, hit me, insulted me, and did many more things to me when I was still a child. This desire increased in me, and I began preparing myself by taking martial arts classes. I obtained a purple belt in Tae Kwon Do. I could go where he was and give him a good thrashing. I accumulated enough money, so that wouldn't be an obstacle. I traveled to Argentina, not on vacation, but to avenge myself. Now, I say because of God's grace and mercy, I never succeeded in finding him.

Hallelujah! Glory to God! Otherwise, instead of writing this book from my home, I would be doing it from prison for having killed him. Once that rejection had been installed in me, roots of bitterness, jealousy, and envy began to grow, which were eventually changed even into death.

If at some moment you have felt rejected by others or self-rejected, it is very important that you pray to God and ask the Holy Spirit to show you the reason for your situation. Let us pray together now: "Heavenly Father, on this day, I renounce the spirit of rejection in my life.

Satan, in Jesus' name, I remove from you the authority that you took in my life. I command you, in the name of Jesus, to leave now and never, ever return. I tear you out of my life in the name of Jesus, and I cast you into the abyss. I now declare myself free of the spirit of rejection. Holy Spirit, thank you for making me free of rejection today.

Chapter 6
I Have to Choose, But I Am Afraid... Whom Do I Follow?

When I had to make the decision of whom to follow, either my "old life" or my "new life," which God was offering me in Christ Jesus, I didn't have any doubts about choosing the "new life." For one simple reason: I had already lived the "old life" for many years and, obviously, I didn't want to live it again. In this, which I call the "old life," I had endured many deceptions. I had been raped, fondled, rejected, and abused.

Adam and Eve's original sin marked humanity for the road of living with Satan.

We believe that sin is something common since it was introduced many years before by means of the disobedience of an "angel." Because sin is something unable to be measured and is accepted as something natural and something that already happened, Satan convinces us to believe, "What else is there to do... it's already been done... there's no way out." So, we continue acting as though nothing will happen, thinking that all is well. This terrible situation has contaminated mankind. What is Satan's purpose? To destroy us completely, beginning with the littlest children up to the adults. We are his target.

But let us not confuse ourselves because this is simple: this is about serving God or serving Satan. We can't serve two gods; we are either with one or the other. I wasn't with God; therefore, I was with Satan. Perhaps you may say that you are not with Satan, but you do the things of this world, thinking that you are pleasing God. I am not one to judge or to say that you are doing good or bad, but if you don't obey God and His commandments, you are obeying Satan. "No one can obey two masters, because he will either hate the one and love the other or he will be devoted to one and despise the other; you cannot serve both God and Mammon." (Matthew 6:24)

For the second time in my life, when I had to choose who to follow, my first reaction was one of fear and trepidation. The spirit of fear was telling me that if I followed Christ, I was going

6. I Have to Choose, But I Am Afraid Whom Do I Follow?

to feel alone. Moreover, I heard a voice in my mind, "You are going to be alone. Your friends, your acquaintances, and close and distant relatives will no longer see or treat you the way they did before. They are not going to love you anymore." Now that I am analyzing my past a little, they were as I was, deceived by Satan. They didn't know the truth. They didn't always do well with me, at least not all the time. In facing my decision, I didn't have much to lose. My friends had failed me sometimes, and others had simply gone away. Boyfriends were at my side for what they could get out of me, and the list went on. All these recollections turned out to be a kind of nourishment if it can be called so, to strengthen me to make the correct decision.

Previously, in this book, I referred to the nature of Satan. If you examine the list, you will find the spirit of fear (the negative faith Adam and Eve received in the Garden of Eden.

That is why I maintain that the one who deposited that fear in me was Satan. In my past, I was beaten, mistreated, raped, and deceived. Fear entered me, and fear is the most common of Satan's principalities. He knows that once we allow that spirit, he can do whatever he wishes with our minds; he deceives us, confuses us, and twists us, placing us in difficult situations, impossible for us to get out of by ourselves. It is at this point that only the help and power of God can free us. From this simple question, knowing who to follow, came a convincing and effective answer. "In love, there is no fear, but perfect love casts out all fear; because fear involves punishment; and the one who fears has not been made perfect in love." (1 John 4:18)

Spritual Blindness

If you ask me, "Why then did you feel lonely if you were going to be in either God's or

Satan's company? I would give you a simple answer: I did not have the discernment to see the truth. Satan places blinders over our eyes, much like a stagecoach driver does to horses, to limit our vision, and he covers our ears so that we can't hear good advice. I was carried away by Satan, living in sin until that glorious moment in which Jesus Christ burst into my life and redeemed me. Jesus Christ removed the bandages from my eyes, and I could see His light. He unplugged my ears, and I could hear the Holy Spirit's beautiful, sweet voice.

Fear blocked my faith. I had no faith because I was afraid. Fear is the opposite of faith. In Eden, Adam said, "I heard your voice in the Garden, and I was afraid because I was naked, and I hid myself." (Genesis 3:16) Fear does not allow us to believe God's word. "Now faith is the assurance of things hoped for, the conviction of things not seen." (Hebrews 11:1) We do not have to see Jesus, we only must have faith, believe in Him, and obey Him. Satan used my first sweetheart to physically abuse me. Satan wanted to destroy me, to kill me so that the plan that God had for me would not be carried out. When we sin against God, we are separated from Him; we no longer have His covering. Satan sees us, that we are uncovered, and he bandages our physical eyes with a spiritual veil that does not permit us to see God's truth anymore - so we believe his lies- we act the way he wishes, committing more errors, ending up completely separated from our Creator. Spiritual death is when we separate ourselves from God; in the physical, we keep on doing the opposite of what God commands, while in the spiritual, we are

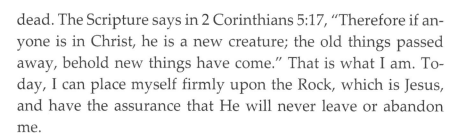

6. I Have to Choose, But I Am Afraid Whom Do I Follow?

dead. The Scripture says in 2 Corinthians 5:17, "Therefore if anyone is in Christ, he is a new creature; the old things passed away, behold new things have come." That is what I am. Today, I can place myself firmly upon the Rock, which is Jesus, and have the assurance that He will never leave or abandon me.

When the moment came to decide whom to follow, I had to make a choice, but I had never seen God, I had never experienced Him, and I was fearful because I had suffered much in the past. It was hard for me to believe that God had the power to change my life completely. I didn't have enough faith to believe Him. Questions came into my mind. Who am I that God would take an interest in me? Can it be that now I am suddenly worth something to Him? Where was He when I was molested? Why didn't He defend me? And a thousand more questions.

Today, I know, and I can tell you that those questions did not even come from me, but they came from Satan (the accuser) and from all his demons so that I couldn't choose who to follow. Who, having the opportunity of this kind or being able to experience something "new/good," would want to continue with the same nightmare? How long must we put up with the devil's tricks? Having been mistreated, we think that God isn't interested in us because we believe that we are worthless. It's hard for us to choose the right way, and we doubt whom to follow. Truthfully, the only thing I ever experienced from Satan was PAIN!

Are you ready to receive this new life that I talked about? Let us pray this prayer together, "Heavenly Father, I recognize that I am a sinner. I come before Your Presence to repent of my sins. I ask you to forgive me in the name of Your son, Jesus Christ, for having disobeyed You. My disobedience separated me from You. Accept me, Lord. I invite you to come into my heart and to be the master of my life and of my being. Father, in the name of Jesus, I ask you to write my name in the book of life. Amen.

Chapter 7
Making a Decision

When making a decision, it is important to be prepared and determined to do it. A decision without action does not have any effect. Many times, we think more about what we are going to do without realizing that we are wasting time. The decision and the preparedness to do it have to be accompanied by an action.

The word "prepared" is the past participle of the verb "to prepare" and from the Latin "dispositus". As an adjective, it can mean:

1) elegant, well proportioned,

2) capable, clear headed. It can be used as "well": with full health, favorable vitality. And as "ill": without health, with adverse energy.

The word "decided" as an adjective means resolved, acting decisively. To be able to succeed in making a change in our life, first, a decision to change must be made: "I want to change." Then you are ready to say. "I am going to do it." Third, to succeed, you must renounce what you were doing before, "I am not going to do this anymore." The word "commitment" means "with willingness. persistence in the execution of something. competing with others. The past participle of "to appoint," which is "appositus" in Latin, is an adjective that means "dressed up, adorned, of gentle disposition in a person. "Dressed up" means to clean up, to consist of, to adorn.

Please forgive me that this sounds a bit complicated, but it is necessary to look for the meaning of these words to clearly understand step by step what God is saying to us. While this may seem a little confusing, God is speaking to your heart. How many times do we want and desire to make decisions, to be ready, and to plan something considering what is correct? We cannot simply make a commitment without action.

The first step that we should take is to decide what we want to do. The second step is to determine how, when, and where what we decided to do will be done. The final step will be putting into action what we have decided and determined to do.

7. Making a Decision

For something to truly change within us, we can't stop with the commitment or the determination. For the change to be evident, we must act differently, behaving in accordance with what we wish to change. Otherwise, nothing will ever be transformed, or you will never be able to obtain a renovation or a complete change.

Three of my four children, nieces and nephews, neighbors, and all those I have had the pleasure of "raising" learned to ride a bicycle at age four. By age five, they were professionals at bicycling, racing through the sidewalks of my city. My youngest son started to practice with his bike when he was four. Unfortunately, he fell on one of his attempts and hurt his knees. Somehow, this injury affected him to the point that he never got on a bicycle again until he was nine years old.

I remember when we were going to the park, and he would sit on the swing while his friends went up and down on their bikes. He would watch them ride, wanting to be able to do the same but not realizing that all he had to do was make the commitment, renounce the fear, and try again.

One day, my sister gave a bicycle to my daughter, and when he saw it, he went up to my husband and whispered in his ear, "Daddy, I want a bicycle." My husband shared my son's wish with me. We bought him a brightly colored bicycle full of decals and engravings. When we returned home, my husband inspected it and put air in the tires. My son asked us to pray that God would protect him. Contemplating his new acquisition, he placed his helmet on his head, identifying himself as a "great bike professional." His decision and determination contributed to his success. He got on his bike, started it, and rode. Though I was running by his side to block him in case he fell, it really wasn't necessary. He kept on going confidently, believing God, and he succeeded!

It is possible, when we are willing and committed, to change "something." When we decide, we are acting upon that readiness. "Disposition" comes from the Latin word which means action and effect of readiness. The word determination comes from the Latin "determinatio" which means the action and effect of determining bravery and courage. When we combine all these meanings, we find that it's not the saying but the doing that enables us to make changes in ourselves.

For example, how many times have you planned to go on a diet because you saw that you had been gaining a few more pounds? When you saw yourself in the mirror, the first thought you had was, "OH, I've gained a few pounds. I have to lose weight!" You reacted positively to your thought; This was an act of commitment. You made the decision to slim down.

A decision without determination and action is not going to be something positive. You are not going to lose weight simply because you made a decision. For you to lose that excess weight, you have to determine what you are going to eat from that day forward by using a completely new diet and adding physical exercises. No doubt it will help you to lose weight and toughen your muscles. Only when we make that commitment and place our body in action will we have a positive effect. Notice the meaning of the word "commitment" mentions "resolve," and this is to carry into practice, to bring to fulfillment.

When we know Jesus, it is not enough only to be ready or to be committed; it is necessary for us to decide and commit with the goal of putting everything into action. For this, we

7. Making a Decision

need to execute and exercise faith so that everything is combined. It will succeed in being placed in order. Your path will be cleaned, and everything in accordance with the way God originally created for you from the beginning will be acceptable and enhanced.

I had the opportunity to play basketball for a club in Argentina. I played for eleven years. In the beginning, I would practice with a great deal of enthusiasm. The more I practiced, the better I played. It took a lot of effort on my part because there were rather difficult techniques besides my nerves, which led me to make a lot of mistakes. I used to throw the ball everywhere. After much practice, I succeeded in having an idea more or less of how to play the game and confront my opponents. It was not easy, especially with players who were taller than me. I was not as tall as the others, but being small and thin was an advantage since I could go everywhere. I ran faster than all the others, and I could jump very high. My height would confuse the opponent, and then I learned to feel useful and accepted myself as God had made me. That's the way God had arranged it from the beginning. He will never make us ashamed because we are His children. He created us individually with different gifts. Always look at yourself as a beautiful design because you were designed by the best artist. Instead of criticizing your design, admire it and value how God created you.

When an artist goes to an art gallery, they go for the purpose of critiquing others' work. They learn to adapt and incorporate the techniques they have not yet done themselves. I don't think that a professional looks at other professionals just to criticize them. When you look at yourself in the mirror, do it with optimism; this will make you feel good since you gave your mind a chance to be positive. If you use the negative part of things, you will not feel very good because when you look in the mirror, you will always find a lot of defects. It is better when you look in the mirror that you think and ask, "How do You see me, Jesus?"

This will make you feel much better since His reply will be, "You are my best design."

Say it with confidence, "I am your best design because I was created by the best artist." Although I played a sport that required a certain height, with the height I had, I was a strong tool on the team.

Every change requires a great effort because it leads us to act in a way totally different from the way we were accustomed to act. I imagine it must have been a drastic change for the disciples when Jesus called them. Suddenly, they had to break their bad habits and renounce the things they had been doing. Although the decision they made to follow Jesus was for their good, they still had to learn to trust in Him.

Peter denied Him three times. Thomas searched for Him everywhere because he could not believe that Jesus had risen from the dead. In other words, Thomas doubted, and then Judas betrayed Him.

If we go farther back in time, we can see Moses. He had to decide and make a commitment when God told him to bring the Israelites out of slavery from the Egyptians.

Imagine that! Moses was called to confront Pharaoh (who thought he was a god). He, who had held the Israelites captive for some four hundred years, was being confronted by a stuttering shepherd.

It is not easy when God demands some drastic changes to be made in our lives. We don't like changes because each change is something new - something that we are not familiar with and not used to doing, even more when it involves confronting situations. Jesus Himself said, "These things I have spoken to you that you might have peace. In the world, you will have tribulation, but be of good cheer; I have overcome the world. (John 16:33).

Everything is possible if we trust Him. Every sickness, pain, suffering, and tears Jesus overcame more than two thousand years ago on Calvary's cross. We must only obey Him, to believe Him, and to know that He will do the impossible. That is why it is necessary to die in the flesh and to depend on God so that He can strengthen us and we can live in the Spirit. Once we believe and accept Jesus, we are no longer a part of this world; we live in this world, but we do not do the things of the world. We look for the things of God's Kingdom because we belong to it. For something to be done, it is necessary to act; nothing should be done only for oneself. God placed us on this earth to do His will, not our own.

Make the decision now and act on it. If you don't know what to do, ask God. He is waiting for you. Remember that you are not alone. He will never leave you nor forsake you. Leave that place in which you are oppressed, captive, enslaved. Get up, and lift your hands to heaven! Satan knows your weakness; he is going to make you act the same way he used Peter when he said, "God forbid it, Lord; this shall never happen to You!"

Spritual Blindness

The scripture needs to be fulfilled as the prophet Isaiah announced it. Let us read together what the word of God says:

"From that time on, Jesus began to declare to His disciples that it was necessary to go to Jerusalem and to suffer many things from the elders and chief priests and scribes; and to be killed and raised up on the third day. Then Peter took Him aside and began to rebuke Him, saying, 'God forbid it, Lord; this shall never happen to You! But He turned and said to Peter, 'Get behind Me, Satan! You are a stumbling block to me, for you are not setting your mind on God's interest, but man's.'" (Matthew 16: 21- 23)

This passage clearly explains to us that Satan does know our weaknesses, and in this way, he knows how to manipulate us. We see that in Peter's weakness, he used him to try to convince Jesus not to go to the cross and so the Scriptures could not be fulfilled. Peter wanted Jesus to have compassion on him so that He would not do the Father's will.

I am referring to weakness as something we desire, something we think we need, or something we think is in our best interest. In this case, I have no doubts that Peter loved Jesus. Obviously, he didn't want Jesus to suffer, but in reality, he was looking at everything with human eyes, not with spiritual eyes. God has a plan and a purpose for us. Our job is to know that plan and purpose. To know them, we must communicate with the Holy Spirit. He will take charge of guiding us to find them. Make your decision today so that God's plan will be fulfilled in your life.

Chapter 8
Don't Delay the Process

In our lives, we have processes. A process is the sequence of actions interlaced and directed to reach a purpose or to pursue the fulfillment of objectives. If this process is intercepted, delayed, or reversed, it can be harmful, and you must renounce it.

Some synonyms for the word process are: cause, summary, argument, judgement, matter, progression, step, race, phase, and development. In every process, there is a cause, a progression, a matter, a phase, a step, a race. The most important thing is to get to the goal. The Apostle Paul says, "I have fought the good fight, I have finished the race, I have kept the faith." (2 Timothy 4:7)

Let us keep in mind that Paul went through many difficult and painful moments, such as tribulations, persecutions, disputes, judgements, being stoned and left for dead, and so on. He said that he had finished the race and, above all, he had kept the faith. He simply believed. He did not dwell on the events of the process, but he carried them to the end together with God as God was telling him.

Through the circumstances of life, we concentrate on difficult moments where our actions make us impatient. We lose our calm, we think time is over for us and that we will not reach our goal, to a completed process.

"But, beloved, do not let this fact escape your notice: that with the Lord, one day is as a thousand years and a thousand years as one day. The Lord is not slow about His promise as some count slowness but is patient toward you, not wishing for any to perish, but for all to come to repentance." (2 Peter 3:8,9)

God created us with a plan and a purpose. We weren't created by him simply to be created. We were created with a purpose of completing a divine plan. Our purpose in life is not merely birth, growth, reproduction, and death. There is much more to life than that. God's plan is for our redemption and eternal life spent in His Kingdom.

We are not meant to compare ourselves with the rest of God's creations. God created us in His "image and likeness."

8. Don't Delay the Process

Comparing ourselves to anything else is like comparing God to anything but Himself. We were formed with His hands giving us His image, His own breath of life, and His essence, which is in us. "The Spirit of God made me; and the breath of the Omnipotent One gave me life." (Job 33:4).

For God, human worth is much more than the worth of a tree or an animal. God created the plants and then the animals. And then, when everything was in its place, He formed man from the dust. He blew the breath of life from His spirit into man. He gave man instructions that were to be fulfilled. Human beings were created with a spiritual mind and a soul, which allows us to have a relationship with the Creator. Animals and plants are here for the purpose of serving us, and they cannot have communication with God.

Man disobeyed God's instructions by sinning against Him and by carrying it to the point that he delayed the process so that it would not manifest the plan and purpose of God in his life. God's plan for mankind will never change, but when we disobey, we delay it.

If we wonder why we feel that we are not prosperous and feel that it is because we are overworked, causing both physical and emotional exhaustion, it is because we have disobeyed God. Disobeying Him is not doing what He wills of us. And without an intimate relationship, it is impossible to communicate with Him.

Sin separates us from the presence of God. We begin to do things according to our own wisdom and knowledge, which, without God, is useless. Everything done without God does not prosper and delays the process.

"Trust in the Lord with all your heart and lean not unto your own understanding. In all your ways acknowledge Him, and He will make your paths straight." (Proverbs 3:5,6)

"But the wisdom that is from above is first pure, then peaceable, gentle, reasonable, full of mercy and good fruits, unwavering, without hypocrisy." (James 3:17)

"Because God gives wisdom, knowledge, and intelligence." (Proverbs 2:6)

"Therefore, be careful how you walk, not as unwise men, but as wise, making the most of your time because the days are evil." (Ephesians 5:15,16)

"If any of you lacks wisdom, let him ask of God, who gives to all generously and without reproach, and it will be given to him." (James 1:5)

We are used to living a life in the circle of existence where we are born, grow, reproduce, and die. During the stage of growth, we go to school, we make friends, and we begin to go down different paths. Some begin a career at a university, some get married, and others have children. We pass through important moments experiencing new things, but these things are the most effective when we do them in God's time or, that is, "within" God's time, that which is already established by Him. When I talk about God's time, I am referring to when He commands, and to know when that true time is, it is necessary for there to be communication with Him. How do we communicate? By inviting Him to be an important part of our lives, by talking to Him sincerely, by becoming His friend, and by confessing our situation to Him, keeping Him in mind within the processes of our lives.

8. Don't Delay the Process

Only when we have a deep intimacy with Him, we can hear His voice. God is always waiting for us. If we do not follow Him, we distance ourselves from Him, and it keeps us from hearing Him until we finally lose complete contact. Draw near to Him to be able to experience that intimacy, to be able to follow and obey Him. When we act on our own knowledge, we are living a life away from what God has planned; it's as if we left the plan that He had for us. That is why we begin to amass pains, delusions, and confusion.

The last example is the cycle of life for every living being, but God's idea was more extensive and broader. When He created the heavens and the earth, He already had a plan for your life and for mine. It was, and it continues to be beautiful. But when I choose a path different from God's path, and I imagine that you also have chosen another path that was not God's, we disobeyed, and our suffering begins by desiring a change now. This change could be identified as a conviction that God has placed in your heart so that you realize that the life you have been leading or the life you are living, which is not God's divine plan, can be changed.

In the Gospel of John, the Bible speaks about Thomas, one of Jesus' disciples. He asked, "Lord, we do not know where You are going. How, then, can we know the way?" Jesus said to him, "I am the way, the truth and the life; no one comes to the Father except by Me. If you knew Me, you would know my Father also; and from now on you know Him and you have seen Him." (John 14: 5-7)

"And we know that God causes all things to work together for good to those who love God and to those who are called according to His purpose." (Romans 8:28). When reading this biblical passage, we realize that in our lives, the past was not in vain, but that God allowed everything, the good and the bad. If we decide to include God at any point whatsoever in this process in our lives, and we give every legality to God, he will take control to show us that all things work together for good. If God allowed your past to be more horrible than it should have been, now He will use it to fill you with blessings and understanding.

We can see this clearly in what Paul said to the Corinthians in one of his letters.

"Now I rejoice, not that you were made sorrowful but that you were made sorrowful to the point of repentance, for you were made sorrowful according to the will of God so that you might not suffer loss in anything through us. For the sorrow that is according to the will of God produces a repentance without regret, leading to salvation, but the sorrow of the world produces death. For behold what earnestness this very thing, this godly sorrow, has produced in you: what vindication of yourselves, what indignation, what fear, what longing, what zeal, what avenging of wrong! In everything you demonstrated yourselves to be innocent of the matter." (2 Corinthian s 7: 9-11)

Paul shares this with the Corinthians after having been saved through Christ. In his skeptical life, Paul hated Christians, and he sought to kill them. This was his past. Note the change in this passage that he himself wrote later in the book of Acts, "Brethren and Fathers, hear my defense which I now offer to you." And when they heard that he was addressing them in the Hebrew dialect, they became even more quiet; he said, "I am a Jew, born in Tarsus of Cilicia, but brought up in

8. Don't Delay the Process

this city, educated under Gamaliel, strictly according to the law of our fathers, being zealous for God, just as you all are today. I persecuted this way to the death, binding and putting both men and women into prison, as also the high priest and all the Council of the elders can testify. From them I also received letters to the brethren and started off to Damascus in order to bring even those who were there to Jerusalem as prisoners to be punished." (Acts 22:1-5)

Paul recognized his sin and testified what he had done in his past. He told them that he was a Jew, but the sin that he was committing was not right in the eyes of God. Thus, even God, seeing all that he was doing, who knew him from his mother's womb, just as He knows you and me. Our heavenly Father knew the plan that He had for Paul, but because of his disobedience, that plan could not be fulfilled until his heart was transformed according to God's will.

From verse eight on, he says, "But it happened that I was on my way, approaching Damascus about noontime, a very bright light suddenly flashed from heaven all around me, and I fell on the ground and heard a voice saying to me, 'Saul, Saul, why are you persecuting Me?' And I answered, 'Who are You, Lord?' And He said to me, 'I am Jesus of Nazareth whom you are persecuting.' And those who were with me saw the light, to be sure, but did not understand the voice of the One who was speaking to me. And I said, 'What shall I do, Lord?' And the Lord said to me, 'Get up and go on into Damascus, and there you will be told of all that has been appointed for you to do.' But since I could not see because of the brightness of the light, I was led by the hand of those who were with me and came into Damascus. A certain Ananias, a man who was devout by the standard of the Law, well-spoken of by all the Jews who lived there, came to me and, standing next to me, said, 'Brother Saul, receive your sight.' And at that very time, I looked up at him; and he said, 'The God of our fathers has appointed you to know His will and to see the Righteous One and to hear an utterance from His mouth, for you will be a witness for Him to all men of what you have seen and heard. Now, why do you delay? Get up and be baptized, and wash away your sins, calling on His name." (Acts 22:6-16)

Pay attention to when Jesus asks Saul, "Why are you persecuting Me?". Jesus was referring to what Paul was doing, persecuting His followers, even to the point of killing them. Why are you persecuting My followers, and why do you want to kill them? Yes, Paul literally killed Christians, followers of Jesus. So, if God's mercy even forgave Saul, how much more will He forgive us if we repent? Can you imagine Paul, the one who became so faithful to God after being saved, who first, in his skepticism, had killed Christians? It's hard to believe, isn't it? But it was that way because only God, through Jesus Christ can do something like that! For us today, Paul is an example of what God did in him in His own time. God wants to do the same thing in us today! There is nothing impossible for God!

The thing that stands out the most to me in Paul's life is that he didn't know Jesus physically. He didn't walk, eat, rest, or speak to Jesus as the disciples had done. He did not have the opportunity to live with Jesus for more than three years. They shared many miracles during that time; they witnessed Jesus doing healings, resurrections, paralytics walking, the blind seeing... even though one of them doubted that Jesus had risen

8. Don't Delay the Process

from the dead, another rejected Him, and another betrayed Him.

'On the road to Damascus, Paul experienced a personal encounter with the Holy Spirit, and he believed. It may be that you are on that road, which is connecting you with the recognition and repentance that bring you the desire to have a new life, completely different from the life you have been living up until this moment.

I doubt that anyone who leaves one life for another is or can, directly or indirectly, become happy. That person is impelled or provoked to commit murder; he is full of bitterness and hatred toward others, full of skepticism, jealousy, or envy, even up to the point of wanting to take his own life.

The bitterness and hate that incites one person to take the life of another increases daily inside of him, leading him to commit murder or suicide. Inside, in his spirit, in his inner being, in his conscience or soul, it is impossible to have a life of peace.

The truth is in the encounter and to recognize that it is necessary to accept, yield to, and believe in Jesus so that your life changes completely. If you have pride, you will never recognize that your soul needs a Savior.

My road to Damascus was when I basically died to pride, and I recognized my physical and emotional state. I accepted Jesus by giving Him the right and the authority to change my life.

My life before getting to know Jesus was simple. I never allowed myself to be carried away by material possessions; I always worked for what I needed, and I had a lovely family. I achieved everything I set out to do with my sacrifice and consistency; I worked hard, and I was rewarded for it. But while I was busy with my life, my things, my family, my job, my house, my car, my desires, "divorce" visited me, causing a great deal of pain and suffering. I came to the point of seeing, feeling, and understanding what deep pain really was. I suffered because my family was destroyed, and my pain was greater when I saw my children suffering.

Later, I understood that God had been calling me for many years to show me what His divine plan was for my life, but I never heard Him, and I preferred to arrange my own affairs in my own way. The Lord is always calling us, and although we want to do things our own way, He never stops seeking us.

I am not saying that God brought the divorce into my life; rather, my disobedience to Him brought me to that horrible phase. I deeply believe that God loves us unconditionally and that only good comes from Him, but the disobedience and sin that is within us will take us to the point of desperation that God will use for us to draw near to Him.

On this day, I stand firmly with the authority that Jesus has given me to tell you, "Do not make the same mistake. Don't wait to become desperate or reach the end of your life to recognize that God is God over everything, and you are not.

Jesus can turn your mourning into dancing. "You have turned my mourning into dancing, you have loosed my sackcloth and girded me with gladness." (Psalm 30:11) He can give life to your desert. "I will open rivers on the bare heights, and springs in the midst of the valleys; I will make the wilderness a pool of water and the dry land fountains of water." (Isaiah

8. Don't Delay the Process

41:18) Accept Jesus now; this is the moment; recognize Him and don't delay the process any longer.

After the divorce, my life became more complicated since I had to fulfill the role of both mother and father. I had more responsibilities with the children, the home, and work. It was very exhausting for me. I began to experience sicknesses in my body, and I ended up with medication for the thyroid, depression, cholesterol, anemia, etc.

Everything got worse each time, and with my sick body, it was hard to keep on going. On one of my visits to the doctor, he recommended that I see a psychologist. I called for an appointment, and the following week, I went to see him. In the doctor's office, waiting to be seen, I became exasperated, and I couldn't breathe. I got tired of waiting. I became angry, and I left that place. When I got outside, I saw snow everywhere, and I began to pick it up with my hands without gloves, placing it on my face, desperately wanting the cold to calm my panic attack that was taking away my breath and making me anxious, feeling palpitations in my throat, manifesting a heart attack. I felt a little better. I went back to the doctor's office and finally got to see the doctor. I followed all his instructions, but my state of mind did not change. The panic attacks kept coming every day. By taking a pill, everything would get calm for a while. Life continued, and the pressures kept increasing. My children were fearful because they saw me in a bad way, but I needed to keep on going.

My son started to have behavior problems in public school, and I decided to take them out of there and enroll them in a private school to give them more discipline. I called the Catholic school near our house, but that did not work because they told me it was the middle of the year, and if they accepted my children, they would distract the rest of the students.

For a moment, I thought the world was falling on top of me. I felt they despised my children. I became exasperated because I had taken them out of school and couldn't find a place to put them. In the United States, it is very important for children to go to school; if they don't go for more than three days, they right away call the parents to find out why the children are not in school. Time went on, and I couldn't find a school that would accept them.

At that moment, I looked out the window of my kitchen, and I saw a building facing my house with a sign that had the name of a private school and the phone number. We had already been living in this house for two years, and every morning, while having my coffee, I would look outside that window, but I never saw the sign or that building. Without a doubt, today, I say that "something " or "someone" (and I refer to the spiritual) was working against me by closing that place or by making that place invisible so I would never see it.

I couldn't believe what I was seeing; I dialed the number and made the call. A very nice young woman took my call. She asked how she could help me, and I told her that my children were not in school. I urgently needed to enroll them to keep from having issues with the state, running the risk that they would take my kids away. She answered me, saying, "Bring them here right away." I quickly enrolled them, and they started going to their classes.

As time went on, I began to have a relationship with the other parents, and I enjoyed talking with them and their nice

8. Don't Delay the Process

children. During one conversation, I found out that it was a Christian school, and in the upper part of the building was the church. Every morning, the teachers and the students would go up to the sanctuary to worship and praise God. Then, they would bring their offerings and prayer requests.

These children between the ages of four and thirteen interceded for their parents, brothers, sisters, cousins, aunts, uncles, and all their family members to be saved. They would also ask Jesus for the salvation of mankind in the entire world! In that moment of prayer, you as well as I, were on that list! God hears everyone and what they pray!

One day, my daughter commented to me that the parents of the other kids went to church on Wednesdays and Sundays. She insisted several times that I go, but I always looked for excuses as to why I couldn't go. She insisted so many times that I finally decided to go. I thought if I went at least once, then she would stop asking me, and I wouldn't have to go anymore.

The first day I did not understand very much of what the pastor was saying, but there was something different that caught my attention. I went to church occasionally to keep myself in good standing with the school, but it didn't interest me very much. I had finally found a way to have peace in my life, and my children had settled into the routine. I started to feel better and continued working.

The medicine was, at that time, my hope of continuing to fight, and my body got used to taking it, but I still didn't feel completely well. One morning, as usual, I got ready to go to work. I got to the office, and I began to feel out of sorts. It wasn't the usual feeling of exhaustion; I had never felt that way before.

I called my boss and asked for permission to go home because I wasn't feeling well. He let me go and asked if I needed someone to take me. I told him no, that I could get home by myself.

I left the place, got to my car, and began to drive. Being on the road, I noticed that my fingers, my hands, and even my arms began to disappear. At that moment, I thought that I was going crazy. I left the highway, parked in a restaurant parking lot, and looked at my hands again. Everything had returned to normal.

At that moment, fear entered me, and I felt alone. I didn't know who to call. I heard a voice that said, "Call the pastor of the church." And I did. The secretary answered the phone. I asked if I could see the pastor. She told me I could. In desperation, on account of what had happened, I made it to the church. I entered his office and stayed there for two hours talking to him.

In time, I understood that while I was on the road, what I was experiencing was not madness. It was an encounter with the Holy Spirit of God! That was my road to Damascus! The prayers of those children had been answered by the Almighty One, bringing salvation to my soul. From then on, Jesus has had the most important place in my life. Now that I have a personal relationship with Jesus, I understand that I was the fruit of the prayers of those children. I shout "Glory to God" every day because I stopped delaying the process!

Chapter 9
Change Your Way of Thinking

Let us start asking God for a mental transformation to change our way of thinking. In this way, we will be free to think and act like Him. Remember that when our mind changes, we will be able to change our habits. A habit is a learned and constantly exercised action. A habit is a custom that can be good and bad at the same time.

Spritual Blindness

As an example, we can look at people who have been hurt in their past. They were despised and mistreated physically and verbally. These people have the tendency to mistreat others, something that is not good. Unfortunately, the only thing they can give is what they have received. It is very common to meet people who constantly produce the mistreatment received in the past.

No human being likes to suffer or to be hurt. When we are attacked physically or verbally, it brands us. We learn a new but wrong form of thinking and acting. We cover ourselves with an armor of hatred, and this makes us distance ourselves from others. By changing our character, we become aggressive, and we want to be right in everything. We speak in a tone superior to others, thinking no one else can be right, only we can; it's what we say, period. It is a way of covering the pain within. Although we are suffering on the inside, we are dressed in a shell, displaying a strong character before others, pretending to be a strong person. In this way, we think we ensure ourselves of not being hurt again. When we have been treated that way, we tend to suffer emotional, physical, and spiritual complications.

There are many examples we can use that cause wounds, such as divorce, the loss of a loved one, or a son or daughter who is on drugs or incarcerated. There are many different cases, but all with the same result. The way our mind and heart can react depends on the circumstance. Although all these cases are very common nowadays, some of us must go through them, and we have a hard time understanding what causes them to happen. We are already suffering physical and emotional sicknesses because of them.

9. Chang Your Way of Thinking

It is interesting that when I was studying God's word, I read the passage about the woman who was bent over, which says as follows:

"And there was a woman who for eighteen years had had a sickness caused by a spirit, and she was bent over and could not straighten up at all. When Jesus saw her, He called her over and said, 'Woman, you are freed from your sickness.'" (Luke 13: 11-12)

According to the Bible, this woman had not been born that way. She was hunched over for eighteen years. The world introduces her as having a spirit of infirmity. In my case, I was not physically bent over, but I was spiritually bent over and very sick. My spirit was weakened, sad, embittered, without a vision, without a purpose to go on, and without any perspective. Being bent over physically or mentally limits you from seeing certain things that are at a determined level of height. For example, the mountains (which represent the height of achievement whether it be at work or in a sport), the horizon (something stable, linear related to others including family), a panorama (something complete, there is no expectation). The whole picture is found at a level greater than the limit of your vision.

Being bent over brings complications. Can you imagine the emotional state of that woman upon finding_ herself in that situation? She was limited, and I think that she, with multiple limitations, would have complications, as in marriage or friendships. She could even have been angry about her life. Thousands of examples could be given to describe this woman in her condition. You and I could be the same way or worse. In my case, since there was nothing_ physically wrong with me, I was

Spritual Blindness

able to hide my spiritual and emotional stooped over condition. But she could not hide it. Obviously, her body made her defect very clear. When Jesus told her, "You are freed from your infirmity," she straightened up, and her body was moved instantly. It changed its position. She was no longer doubled over with her head bowed toward the ground but found herself in a totally erect position. In this way, she could see everything around her perfectly without any limitation whatsoever. Jesus' miracle in her was done and verified. She was straightened. Why did Jesus say, "Woman, you are freed"? It was necessary for Jesus to say this to her because He was referring to her mind. He was speaking to the spirit of her mind. It was the only way of being able to change her because the body responds according to the spirit of our mind.

When we have a healthy spirit, our mind, our heart, and body are healed as well. Jesus had to change her mind because she would never have been able to accept or understand her healing. It was necessary for Jesus to free her way of thinking because otherwise, she would have gone crazy and would never have understood what had happened.

"I will hear what God the Lord will say, because He will speak peace to his people, to His godly ones so that they will not turn back to their folly. (Psalm 85:8)

"But the natural man does not accept the things of the Spirit of God, for they are foolishness to him, and he cannot understand them, because they are spiritually discerned." (I Corinthians 2:14)

When she was healed mentally, the shape of her body changed in an instant, and she understood and accepted her

9. Chang Your Way of Thinking

healing. Are you stooped over at this time? How much pain are you carrying on your shoulders? How heavy is your load?

Jesus doesn't ask her all these questions; He just says to her, "You are freed of your sickness," and he is saying the same thing to you currently. You aren't bent over anymore. Leave the anger, the depression, the sadness, the hate. Tell yourself this, "I am freed because Jesus has made me free." And in this way, you will be able to have a new mind.

This new mind is a spiritual mind. Hand it over to Jesus, and He will do work on you. Don't concern yourself with what may be oppressing you; straighten up and walk with your head held high, with faith, courage, and joy. Change your way of thinking. "Do not be conformed to this world but be transformed by the renewing of your mind so that you may prove what the will of God is, that which is good, acceptable, and perfect." (Romans 12:2)

"But You, 0 LORD, are a shield about me, my Glory and the one who lifts my head. I cried unto the LORD with my voice, and He answered me from His holy mountain." (Psalm 3:3- 4)

At this time, I feel the need to pray for you. It is not by chance that you are reading this book. Therefore, read this prayer aloud.

"Heavenly Father, at this time, I recognize that my behavior has not been agreeable to You, and I ask You to forgive me of all my sins. Holy Spirit, help me to see the root of my condition; show me exactly the area that is affecting my life. Clean and heal me on the inside so that on the outside, I can show everyone Your presence in me. Heal my soul and lift my head so I can see straight ahead and walk in your ways. Forgive me for having offended others, and I forgive everyone who has offended me. I place these sins under the powerful blood of Jesus Christ. Satan, I remove your hold on my life and that of my family. I cast you into the deepest part of the oceans where nothing can survive. In the name of Jesus. Amen."

Now, the Holy Spirit will speak to you. Be sure to listen to Him and pay attention to what He is telling you. This way, you will be able to see your affected area. Some problems begin in the mother's womb or at the moment of conception. Ask the Holy Spirit to take you and show you what happened at that moment. Other problems may have their origin during the first years of your life due to hurtful words that were spoken to you by your parents, relatives, or teachers. They did not know the power they had to speak into your life, causing confusion, pain, frustration, insecurity, anger, bitterness, fear, or any other negative emotion to which you have grown accustomed in your life and you have not been able to erase them. Or even worse, you have not been able to recognize them to eliminate them and achieve a healthy and prosperous mind. God is waiting for you. He wants to bless you and change your way of thinking, but you must want it.

Chapter 10
Jesus' Sacrifice on the Cross and the Power of the Blood He Shed

God is not after our sins; He is after our hearts. When we realize that we are sinners, He forgives us and saves us from all sin; that is, He redeems us. The word "redeem" in Greek means "purchase." When we accept Christ in our hearts as Lord and Savior, He redeems us, and we become His own.

In ancient times, when a slave was bought, it was a transaction to redeem him from his present master, and he would never belong again to the one who sold him. Generally, but not in every case, the slave had to work for and serve his new master. Nowadays, we could use the example of going to the market. We buy something, and we own what we buy. We acquire something by paying for the item we want. We take it off the shelve to either use it, present it as a gift, or for some other use. The fact is that the item purchased no longer belongs to the one who used to own it.

When Jesus died on the cross, He did it for the purpose of freeing mankind from the power of sin and everything else that would enslave us. He redeemed us from the captivity of the devil by succeeding in making us free eternally. The crucifixion of Jesus was necessary. The prophecy had to be fulfilled. When Jesus was on the cross, everyone looked at Him, mocked Him, and some said, "He saved others; let Him save himself, if this is the Messiah, the chosen one of God." (Luke 23:35)

Upon making that declaration, they were hoping that Jesus would give in to not fulfilling God's will but would fall into the sin of disobedience to the Father. They were not only provoking Him when they said, "Save yourself," but they also gave Him vinegar to drink. Now, to what thirsting man do you give vinegar to quench his thirst? They also took his clothes and cast lots for them. On the top of the cross, they placed the title saying, "THIS IS THE KING OF THE JEWS." Everything was a mockery. They were provoking Him so that He would fall into sin. Glory to God! Jesus overcame sin on the cross because He trusted in the Father and did not disobey Him. "But he was wounded for our transgressions, crushed for our iniquities; the

10. Jesus' Sacrifice on the Cross and the Power of the Blood He Shed

punishment for our peace (wellbeing) fell upon Him, and by his stripes we are healed. (Isaiah 53:5)

How many times have you been provoked, insulted, pushed, scorned? Let me tell you that of everything that has been done to you, nothing can compare to Jesus' suffering on the cross of Calvary. He did not do this so we could say, "How amazing was this man!". No, He did not make this sacrifice to impress others. He did it because the scriptures had to be fulfilled so that, in this way, mankind could be saved and freed from sin. Anyone who does not accept Jesus in their hearts will never get to the heavenly Father. He did it so that you and I might be cleansed from all sin when our moment (death) arrives. We can dwell with our heavenly Father throughout eternity.

Condemnation does not come from God. Satan condemns us after we have sinned, but God convicts us in our hearts to recognize that what we did is wicked in His eyes.

Remember, God is holy, and therefore, sin separates us from His presence. Many people say, "If I could only change my past!." Our past is a reflection of the present. If we change the past, we will have double work. First, to get to know a new past, and then to work harder for the present because we don't have enough experience from the past. We cannot cancel or change what already was. Let us use the past to have a better present. Let us recognize our mistakes. Let us use all the elements at our disposal for power today to do things in the correct way. Now is the time to act, reconcile, unite ourselves to God, and have an opportunity to make it right. "To everything there is a season, and there is a time for every event under heaven." (Ecclesiastes 3:1)

To truly understand the sacrifice Jesus made on the cross, let us look at the Old Testament, where it speaks of how God used the sacrifice of the blood of the lamb as a representative of Jesus. When God made Adam and Eve, He gave them only one command that they could not do inside of Eden; even so, they disobeyed. When God created Eden, everything He made was good. Everything God created was good because God is good. He is love. God created us in His likeness; He desired His own perfect creation. Then, when they sinned, disobeying God, they were thrown out of Eden. Creation didn't stay good. God had to cover that sin by killing one of His creations, that is, an innocent animal. That is where the fall of man on earth began, and sin became common.

God cursed the earth because of the disobedience of the man used by Satan to bring sin into this world. In the book of Genesis, chapter 4 tells us what happened with Cain and Abel, Adam and Eve's first sons.

"Now the man had relations with his wife Eve, and she conceived and gave birth to Cain, and she said, 'Now I have gotten a man-child with the help of the Lord.' Afterward she gave birth to his brother Abel. And Abel was a keeper of flocks, but Cain was a tiller of the ground." (Genesis 4:1-2)

Cain was the firstborn son of Adam and Eve (the first son born of a man and a woman). When Cain and Abel had to bring an offering to God, evidently, God favored Abel's offering since it was related to the blood of a lamb.

10. Jesus' Sacrifice on the Cross and the Power of the Blood He Shed

"And it came about in the course of time that Cain brought an offering to the Lord of the fruit of the ground. Abel, on his part, also brought the firstlings of his flock and of their fat portions. And the Lord looked with favor on Abel and on his offering. But for Cain and his offering He had no regard. And Cain became angry and his countenance fell. (Genesis 4:3-5)

Cain was saddened and angry and decided to kill his brother Abel in a fit of jealousy. Notice how terrible it is to be jealous, and I ask myself, where does jealousy come from? Why do we feel jealousy if we were all created equal with the same proportions and likeness of God? Well, remember, the devil came to kill and destroy us spiritually, and he was the one who provoked and induced man to sin simply so that God's plan would not come to pass. The intentions of the two brothers were good. Both of them brought an offering to God in accordance with their livelihood. The farmer brought grain, and the shepherd brought an animal because he raised animals. However, God only looked with favor on the blood of the animal.

Because we are impatient and disobedient, and we don't like to be rejected by anyone, the same scenario happens today. Perhaps we get jealous of our brothers or sisters. When jealousy entered Cain's heart, it was then when the devil took possession of him because Cain opened a door, and Satan tempted him to kill his brother. Incidentally, jealousy passed through Lucifer when he saw God creating man. This jealousy transformed him into Satan.

"God asked Cain where his brother was and Cain said that he didn't know. But God, when he didn't get the truth from Cain, searching for the blood of Abel, asked him, 'What have

Spritual Blindness

you done? The voice of your brother's blood cries out to me from the ground. Now then may you be cursed from the ground which has opened her mouth to receive your brother's blood from your hand." (Genesis 4: 10-11) Then God cursed Cain because of what he had done to his brother.

Blood is very meaningful because it blots out every sin, including the original sin of Adam and Eve, the same sinful nature that we inherit from the time we are born. It is for this reason that God sent Jesus to save us from that original sin and all our other sins as well. It is the blood of Jesus which blots out every sin, covers us, and cleanses us. Maybe you have never reached the point of killing or handing over an innocent person to the authorities. However, in your life, you have done something that was wicked in the eyes of God, and I say this because we are not righteous.

Do you know why we fall into sin? Simply because of little or lack of understanding of the things of God. "My people are destroyed for lack of knowledge." (Hosea 4:6).

"Neither give opportunity to the devil." (Ephesians 4:27)

"Put on the whole armor of God so that you can stand firm against the snares of the devil." (Ephesians 6:11)

When the time for Jesus was approaching, He knew that one of the twelve was going to betray Him. "Jesus answered them, haven't I chosen you, the twelve; and yet one of you is a devil?"(John 6:70). God knows beforehand what we are going to do; it is necessary for these things to happen so that we return to God. "And they may come to their senses and escape

10. Jesus' Sacrifice on the Cross and the Power of the Blood He Shed

the snare of the devil, having been held captive by him to do his will." (2 Timothy 2:26)

When I met Christ and accepted Him in my heart, I remember my pastor talking about the Ten Commandments. At that time, I believed that I had repented of all my sins, which, in fact, was not true. The word "commandment" means that which is imposed by decree or law. In Deuteronomy 5, it talks about the Ten Commandments and in verse 7 it says, "Thou shalt not kill." When I read this, I felt a great pain in my heart, and I began to think more deeply. Before knowing Christ, I had responded to a believer that I was fine and that I didn't need to know about God because I thought that I had never done anything bad to anyone and I had never stolen or killed. Surely, my knowledge of God was very poor. I was unaware of many biblical truths about God. When I met God and began to read the Bible, I realized that I had killed; an abortion is murder. If, in this moment, you think that you are free from sin, you are deceived. We all have sins. We all need to confess them with true repentance. Ask Jesus for a revelation so that you can see your sin, and let us say the following prayer together:

"Heavenly Father, I ask You at this time to forgive me for all my sins, those I remember and those I don't remember. I ask You, Lord, to have mercy on me for everything I have done (here you tell God what your sins are) and that the blood of Jesus may erase (blot out) all my faults; I ask it all in the name of Jesus. Amen.

Chapter 11
A Real Brokenness

The Bible tells us a story about a woman who was a sinner. This passage could be very useful for us since it can be used as an example for our life.

"Then a woman from the city, who was a sinner, when she learned that Jesus was reclining at the table at the at the Pharisee's house, brought an alabaster vial of perfume; and standing behind Him at His feet, crying, she began to wet His feet with tears and wiping them with her hair; she kept kissing His feet and anointing them with perfume." (Luke 7:37-38)

When we read "was a sinner," this shows us that she did not know Jesus, but she wanted to come to Him. Surely, she had heard who Jesus was on account of the comments of others, but she never had a personal relationship with Him. When she learned about the wonders and miracles that Jesus did, she wanted to experience a miracle in her life. She could no longer keep living in her present condition. The truth is that to get to Jesus voluntarily, she had to recognize that she was a sinner, and this led her to repentance. When she recognized her spiritual state, obviously, her pride fell, and she did the impossible, which was to prostrate herself at Jesus's feet.

Why do I say "the impossible?" Because back in those days, men would meet men only, and women could not be in their company. Here, we see that they weren't ordinary men but rather Pharisees (religious legalists). For her to be in that place, she ran the risk that they might punish or even kill her.

Here, we see how a woman repenting of her sins approached Jesus, crying, and her tears fell at His feet. With her hair, she dried those tears, and then she poured perfume on His feet.

She overlooked everything and everyone without it mattering to her what anyone said or thought. She recognized who Jesus was; she saw Him because when she repented, the veil fell from her eyes. Her desire was so great that she completely overlooked the entire situation and just sat near the One who, in an instant, would change her life forever.

Wealthy people think that they don't need Jesus because they have everything they need. They think that a house, expensive cars, food, name-brand clothing, vacations, and a good job are everything they need in this life. It's not a bad thing because God wants us to prosper and have a good income. God's word speaks about prospering. It says that every worker is worthy of his wages. It's not bad to have wealth, but it's more important to have your soul saved so that you can go to heaven instead of going to hell. It can be that wealth may give you a comfortable life on this earth, but all this will remain here. When our time comes, we will take absolutely nothing with us. Jesus died on the cross to save mankind's souls and to set them free from sin.

"It is easier for a camel to pass through the eye of a needle than for a rich man to enter the kingdom of God." (Mark 10:25)

I have had the opportunity to minister to wealthy people, people of means who would say, "I know that God exists, and I pray to Him." They always want me to agree with them that it's good that they believe in God, but for God to hear their prayers, it is necessary to accept God's Son in their heart and to begin a personal relationship with Jesus. Because He is the Savior of our souls, He is interceding for us at the right hand of the Father. Jesus said, "I am the way, the truth, and the life; no one comes to the Father except by Me." (John 14:6). We all need Jesus so that our souls do not go to hell.

This sinful woman was one of the economic means. The alabaster vial was the material with which they used to make very valuable bottles; they sculpted them by hand. The perfume was "pure nard," which was taken from a flower found only on the highest part of a mountain; it took about four days

11. A Real Brokenness

to get these flowers on foot. To obtain the perfume, these flowers had to be crushed. Only someone of economic means could get something of such value. She poured her most valuable possession over the feet of Jesus.

In this passage, there are three personalities: the first or most important main character is Jesus, then the sinful woman, and the Pharisee. The Bible tells us that this woman with the most expensive perfume came to where she found Jesus. She cried in brokenness and prostrated herself at His feet. When we get to the point where we find no motivation, happiness, or stability, and we don't know where to go or what to do because nothing satisfies us, we have no choice but to be broken and come to His feet.

Suddenly, we find everything dark, hazy, and without hope or desires. We no longer see the colors of flowers as we used to, and we no longer talk about smelling the fragrance of the roses. A great despondency invades us, and nothing attracts us. The sky that we used to see is no longer the same color, and we don't even take the time to look up to see what kind of day it is.

It is there when we stop for a moment and ask ourselves, "What is going on? Why don't I feel like I used to feel? Why have I lost all motivation? Before, I used to like to fix myself up and look presentable, and now I don't really care whether I fix myself up or not!" You just need to humble yourself before Him, at His feet.

She found peace, compassion, and the love that brought her to the act of giving Him her all, leaving everything unguarded. In the same way, God wants us to fully surrender to

Him without keeping anything back. He wants us broken before Him so He can make us new by changing everything ugly into something beautiful, every grief into joy, and all suffering into rejoicing.

The pouring out of the perfume shows us that we can come near and even lay our most valuable possessions at His feet and be certain that there is nothing more valuable than He is. Everything that may be in our heart like grief, disillusionment, sadness, let us turn them over to Him.

When this woman desperately cried, her tears fell at Jesus' feet, pouring out all the suffering inside of her. She made contact with Jesus, and not only did He heal her pain, but He also cleansed her from all her sins. She used her hair to dry His feet (remember that in those times, a woman's hair was the most glorious part of her body, and she would use it as a covering. (1 Corinthians 11:15). She used her hair to dry and clean the lowest part of His body, His feet. Why did she concentrate so much on the feet of Jesus? This woman could have used the perfume on Jesus' head or the uppermost part of His body. Instead, she was focused, she was surrendered, and she prostrated herself at His feet. That very repentance took her to where Jesus' authority was, with respect to the demons, because He had them and has had them under His feet for centuries. The brokenness of this woman allowed her to have the sensitivity to see where that authority was residing.

Unfortunately, the Pharisee in this true story is not as sweet as the person we see in the sinful woman because the Pharisee, in certain ways, had doubts as to who Jesus was.

11. A Real Brokenness

"And when the Pharisee who had invited Him saw this, he said to himself, "If this man were a prophet, he would know who and what kind of woman is the one who is touching him, that she is a sinner." (Luke 7:49)

How many times do we take our eyes off Jesus to focus on things which are not important. How many times do we criticize others or complain about personal situations or those of others? There is only one way of eliminating these bad habits. We simply must focus on Jesus. Let us place our eyes on Him, and when we look at others, let it be to bless and not criticize them. Maybe the Pharisee felt he was in the position to say something or make a comment because he didn't have the same courage as the sinful woman to come to the feet of Jesus; perhaps his pride wouldn't let him do it.

It is very important to pay attention to these passages because they will help you to open your heart, recognize your sins, and surrender everything to Him because only Jesus can repair it and heal it. He did not go to the cross in vain. He went to redeem our sins and save our souls so we could receive eternal life with God the Father. May we not be like the Pharisee who perhaps lost his chance of salvation because of concentrating more on the sinful woman and doubting Jesus.

It is easier to see the errors of others because that is where our eyes focus, and they bring to mind a thought related to what we see, and then we judge. Let us use our eyes to look at Jesus in order to look at ourselves. Let us focus on our heart and not on that of another. In this way, we can concentrate on Jesus and become more united to Him, and thus be able to benefit ourselves from His victory on the cross.

Don't place your confidence in things like wealth, leaders, humans, or work. "Those who trust in their wealth and boast in the abundance of their riches, none of them in any way can redeem his brother nor give to God a ransom for him." (Psalm 49:6,7)

Place your trust in the name that is above every name, the name of Jesus, in His word, and in the true God.

"Therefore, our heart rejoices in Him because we have trusted in His holy name." (Psalm 33:21)

Seek Him until you can prostrate yourself at His feet and experience a real brokenness in your life.

Chapter 12
It's My Life and I'll Live It as I Wish

"For men will be lovers of self, lovers of money, boastful, arrogant revilers, disobedient to parents, ungrateful, unholy, unloving, irreconcilable, malicious gossips, without self-control, brutal, haters of good, treacherous, reckless, conceited, lovers of pleasure rather than lovers of God, holding to a form of godliness, although they have denied its power. Avoid such men as these." (2 Timothy 3:2-5). When we do not obey God, we begin to exhibit selfish behavior. The dictionary describes the word selfish as a self-centered person who places his own interests above those of others.

He is a person who is only concerned with himself and his needs. God shows us selfish people in the Bible. The following is a list of examples in the Bible with respect to self-centered behavior:

1 Samuel 17:4-11 (Goliath)

1 Samuel 23:3-11 (Nabal)

Esther 6:6-12 (Haman) Ecclesiastes 2:10-11(Solomon)

Isaiah 14:13-15 and Luke 4:5-6 (Satan) Mark 10:35-37 (James and John

Luke 12:16-21 (The Rich Fool)

Luke 16:19-25 (The Rich Man) John 6:26 (The Jewish People) Acts 20:20-23 (Herod)

3 John 9-10 (Diotrephes)

The above-mentioned list gives examples in the Bible relating to a selfish character, and the following are examples that show its consequences:

Proverbs 23:21 (Poverty)

Romans 13:13-14 (Sin)

Galatians 5:16-17 (Loss of spirituality)

While we think we are doing what is right according to our own understanding, it is not right according to God. How can we think that we are correct in our decisions when we do not

12. It's My Life and i'll Live it as I Wish

consult God? "To consult" means that we read the Book of Instructions (the Bible). It will help us to act correctly. I remember when my father said to me one day, "You do not rule yourself." At that time, I didn't understand what he was referring to. That is, I thought he was referring to the fact that I was under his authority, when in reality, a young man or woman does not like to be under anyone's authority, much less that of their parents. I think that he was referring to God's authority because one day, we are going to have to give God an account of what we did in our lives. "So then, each of us will give an account of ourselves to God."(Romans 14:12)

When I was young, many times I said, "It's my life, and I'll do with it whatever I please because, whether you like it or not, I am going to do what I like, period." What a shame to think that way, don't you think so, too? Why don't we realize that we only hurt ourselves in the end?

When I look at creation, the landscapes, the people, the animals, I see the magnificence of the "designer" who created the best of existence within only six days. The human being is, without a doubt, God's most important and most distinguished masterwork, forming them, with such love and care, in His own image and likeness.

Without desiring to, we were beaten throughout our lives, we have bled and suffered, and we have even hurt others. Something stronger in us controls us, and we start acting selfishly, thinking that we are even the owners of our bodies and our actions. We don't belong to ourselves because we didn't create ourselves. We were created because it pleased the Creator. One day, He saw everything in disarray, and He placed it in order.

"Remember that the Lord is God; he made us and not we ourselves; we are His people and the sheep of His pasture. (Psalm 100:3)

But whim, pride, curiosity, and even ignorance and a little knowledge changed everything. God, the designer and creator, closed the gates of Eden and threw them out. But this did not change His plan; rather, it was that the rebellion would bring consequences. Glory to God because of those who repent and look for God and are instructed with His Holy Word!

How can we change the design of a fashion designer? Likewise, how can we change God's plan? A designer thinks about a design, a style and puts it on paper to visualize it. Once the designer visualizes his design, he transfers it to the fabric he is going to use with the best tones of different colors. This design is already thought of for a specific use, a purpose, or a plan that the designer had in mind before designing it. This cannot be changed or used for something completely different from what it was planned to be. He already has his cuts, his seams, and other things that are going to bring this design to the final stage.

Imagine how this person would feel after having invested so much time and effort in a product when someone comes along and starts to change it. This design is no longer original and, therefore, loses all value and cannot function the way it was designed. We cannot ignore God and think that we ourselves are greater than He is. If we ignore Him, we will fall into sin and lose the value that we have - the design, the plan that

12. It's My Life and i'll Live it as I Wish

was created for us from the beginning, before creation. Our own thoughts and actions are going to lead us to sin, and sin is death. That is the nature we were born with. Therefore, obeying God is the gateway to freedom.

Lucifer was an angel created by God with his magnificent beauty, chosen to worship and please Him.

...You were the seal of perfection, full of wisdom and perfect in beauty. You were in Eden, the garden of God; every precious stone was your covering: the ruby, the topaz, and the diamond; the beryl, the onyx, and the jasper; the lapis lazuli, the turquoise and on the day that you were created they were prepared. You were the anointed cherub who covers, and I placed you there. You were on the holy mountain of God; you walked in the midst of the stones of fire. You were blameless in your ways from the day you were created until unrighteousness was found in you. By the abundance of your trade, you were filled internally with violence, and you sinned. Therefore, I have cast you as profane from the mountain of God. And I have destroyed you, 0 covering cherub, from the midst of the stones of fire. Your heart was lifted up because of your beauty; you corrupted your wisdom by reason of your splendor. I cast you to the ground; I put you before kings that they may see you. By the multitude of your iniquities in the unrighteousness of your trade, you profaned your sanctuaries. Therefore, I have brought fire from the midst of you; it has consumed you, and I have turned you to ashes on the earth in the eyes of all who see you. All who know you among the peoples are appalled at you; you have become terrified, and you will cease to be forever. (Ezekiel 28:12- 19)

Spritual Blindness

Notice the qualities that God gave to Lucifer, with one function, one plan, one job to perform, that compared to the other angels, he was the most distinguished - a position given with the sole end of glorifying God. Nevertheless, Lucifer noticed (enter pride) everything that had been given to him. He intended to use it for his own glory. You could say, "With all this, who needs God!" God created music so we can worship Him. Let's use it for that purpose.

Let us not use the music to give glory, fame, and power to anyone else, especially the devil. In this world, much music is used in a sinful, seductive, tempting way. You can say, "But there are some songs that have good lyrics." This is not about good or bad lyrics; it's about worshiping God and not Satan. Not to mention the songs that say, 0 Momma this... or O Momma that..." with sensual background. When God created Lucifer, He did not create him to be his enemy or adversary. He created him to serve and please Him. Incidentally, he created him beautiful. But when he realized his beauty, he disobeyed God and was thrown out of heaven. We do the same thing when we take the attitude as Lucifer or the thought of saying, "If I have everything, what do I need God for!" or "It's my life, and I will live it the way I want!" "Again I tell you, it is easier for a camel to go through the eye of a needle than for someone who is rich to enter the kingdom of God."(Matthew 19:24)

"How you have fallen from heaven, 0 star of the morning, son of dawn! You have been cut down to the earth, you who have weakened the nations! But you said in your heart, "I will ascend to heaven, I will raise my throne above the stars of God, and I will sit on the mount of assembly in the recesses of the

12. It's My Life and i'll Live it as I Wish

north. I will ascend above the heights of the clouds; I will make myself like the Most High. Nevertheless, you will be thrust down to Sheol, to the recesses of the pit. Those who see you will gaze at you. They will ponder over you, saying, "Is this the man who made the earth tremble, who shook the kingdoms, who made the world like a wilderness and overthrew its cities, who did not allow his prisoners to go home? All the kings of the nations lie in glory, each in his own tomb. But you have been cast out of your tomb like a rejected branch, clothed with the slain who are pierced with a sword, who go down to the stones of the pit like a trampled corpse. You will not be united with them in burial, because you have ruined your country, you have slain your people. May the offspring of evildoers not be mentioned forever." (Isaiah 14:12-20)

Satan is ruling the world we are living in with all his demons. Do not do the same thing that Lucifer did. Notice how many famous people have lost eternal lives by looking for popularity, money, and fame. God bestows gifts upon them, and when they see what they have, they leave God's presence. Remember that everything that departs from God dies. They, too, are cut off from the earth. When we cut a branch from a tree, it dies. While the branch is attached to the trunk, it will be nourished, and it will bring forth shoots so that, later on, fruits can be produced.

This was the plea for Israel to return to the Lord: "Return, O Israel, to the LORD your God, for you have stumbled because of your iniquity. Take words with you and return to the LORD. Say to Him, 'Take away all iniquity and receive us graciously, that we may present the fruit of our lips." (Hosea 14:1-2)

Understand that the one giving the command is God. He sees everything that you do, and today, His beloved Son, the one who died for you and me, the beloved Jesus, says to you now, "Come to me! I do not condemn you. I forgive you. My Father has commanded me so that everyone who believes and confesses that I am the way, the truth, the life, and the Savior will have eternal life!"

Chapter 13
Face the Situations

We know that we are going through some very difficult times. All areas of life are being affected economically, emotionally, culturally, and spiritually. We see how fast life passes us by. Our patience is at an end. Suddenly, we want to throw in the towel, to end everything, and just give up. Women were created with a different emotional makeup than men. Women are expressive, perhaps too demonstrative, possess feelings,

Spritual Blindness

can be overemotional, become sad, joyful, and undoubtedly, very sensitive.

Maybe due to situations we have gone through or those that are happening to us now, we feel the need to show ourselves to be strong before others. Because of our sensitivity, we tend to hide things to avoid arguments or conflicts involving friends, parents, children, family, and even work. We do it this way simply so we do not suffer consequences without realizing that we are committing a mistake. In reality, we are just not facing the matter at hand. That is when we find ourselves with never-ending problems, and we do not know how to manage these conflicts.

These things must be faced regardless of how painful, good, or bad they may be. Confrontation is always the better choice. By nature, we don't like to suffer. Good things are easy and comfortable to deal with. It is very important not to hide the bad; instead, face it. When we find ourselves in a disagreeable situation, we are going to have a chance to express ourselves and make the conflict clear. In that way, the problem is solved, and the situation changes for the good.

I know of a mother who, I'm not sure, tells her children to do their homework after school. But I do know that if they don't do their homework the next day, she doesn't make them go to school. She shouldn't do this because it is not teaching her children discipline. She must teach them to do the homework and go to school because, if they don't do it, they will go to school without the work completed the next day, and they will face the consequences of the decision to not do the homework.

13. Face the Situation

Now, you may say, "They are just kids; they are too young to decide." Well, children make other decisions, so let's teach them what is right and to make good decisions now. A teacher doesn't give students homework they can't do because she already explained it in school; therefore, they know how to do it. Homework basically is practice for what was learned that day. If we cover for our children the way that mom does, teaching them irresponsibility, when they become adults, they will fail at their jobs, as well as in their daily lives, and even with their families. When they have to go to work to support themselves or their family, they won't do it and will use all kinds of excuses not to go to work.

God's teaching prepares us, day by day, to be able to face situations in our lives by using His teaching and putting it into practice every day. It helps us to have the type of life that God has for us, which is to obey and believe Him. Our heavenly Father is not going to give us or ask something of us that we cannot do. Always remember that nothing is impossible for God. To be able to face situations, it is very important to know who God is and the place that we give Him in our lives. For us to be sure that we are not alone, He gives us power and authority to confront every situation.

"And looking at them, Jesus said, For men this is impossible, but for God everything is possible." (Matthew 19:26)

When Jesus called the disciples, they followed Him because they trusted Him. They had faith that Jesus would be able to make a change in their lives. In the book of Hebrews, we can find in chapter 1, verse 1, "Now faith is the assurance of things hoped for, the conviction of things not seen." The disciples were hoping to receive a change in their lives, something better than what would have happened had they not followed Him. For this, it was necessary for them to believe in Him.

What is more, the people of Israel were anxiously waiting for the promised Messiah to have "a change." The word "believe" in Greek is "pisteuo." To believe also means to be persuaded about, and to trust in, to be confident in. In this sense of the word, it means "to lean on, not just a mere belief." (Strong, J 2002)

Believe in Jesus and have faith in Him. Notice when Jesus was teaching the disciples, He compared faith to a mustard seed. Why do you think He chose the smallest of all seeds? "When the crowd got there, a man came to Him and knelt before Him saying: 'Lord, have mercy on my son, who is a lunatic, and he suffers greatly; many times he falls into the fire and many times into the water. And I have brought him to your disciples, but they have not been able to heal him.' 'Answering them, Jesus said, 'Oh, unbelieving and perverse generation! How long shall I be with you? How long shall I put up with you? Bring him here to me.' And Jesus rebuked the demon which came out of the boy, and he was healed from that hour. Then the disciples came to Him privately and said, 'Why could we not drive it out?' Jesus said to them, 'Because of your little faith; for truly I say to you, if you have faith the size of a mustard seed, you will say to the mountain, 'Move from here to there,' and it will move, and nothing will be impossible to you.'" (Matthew 17:14-20)

A mustard seed is one of the smallest, but when the mustard tree grows, it is one of the largest trees that you can imagine. Jesus says that if you have faith like a mustard seed, whatever you need will be done in a mighty way. Do not look at

13. Face the Situation

your situation as a mustard tree. Look at your situation as the size of a mustard seed because if your faith is like the seed, and you place your faith in Jesus, He will do great miracles for you. We have authority and power in the name of Jesus, and that's why it is absolutely important for us to accept Him as the master of our hearts and to serve Him with all our minds, hearts, and souls.

Many years ago, before I met Jesus, I felt the desire to go back to school and finish my college studies. When we have a desire to do something good, that is when the enemy attacks and begins to flood our minds with negative thoughts. In my case, this desire was accompanied by a negative interference saying to me, "You are not sufficient or capable of attending a university because you don't have the ability to learn, and you are already at an advanced age." Today, I say, "Glory to God!" for not having paid attention to that "little voice," although it wasn't easy for me since I was a single mother raising a five-year-old boy and a three-year-old girl. At the university, there was a school for children. Every morning, I would leave my children in their care. I did it for two and a half years to get my associate degree in radio and television. I could not finish. Unfortunately, with only two subjects left, I broke a leg, and it was difficult for me to continue. Then, I got married and had two more children. Therefore, I had no more time to complete my college education.

Before I broke my leg, I met Jesus. He had always been calling me, but I was so occupied with how to fix my life that I had no time for Him. Today, I think how much time and tiredness would have been saved if I had opened the door of my heart before. After twelve years, on the first of January, I heard the voice of the Holy Spirit saying, "All that I started I finished; I created everything in six days, and on the seventh day I rested."

Did you start something that you have never finished? Because if that is so, the Lord wants you to finish it, not to leave anything undone. For you to rest, you must finish what you started. Maybe the enemy has put it into your head saying, "You are already old, you can't study anymore or concentrate on books, you can't memorize, you can't do anything anymore!" Today, I am telling you that you can do anything with faith in the Lord. "Then Jesus said, looking at them, for men it is impossible, but for God no; all things were possible with God."(Matthew 19:26)

I thought that it was impossible for me to finish my college career. Twelve years had passed. I was older, my husband was taking some courses, and the children needed me to help them with their homework. Then, I heard His voice saying, "You can do it because I am with you, and it is necessary for you to finish what you started so that I can use you." When I heard God speaking to me, I didn't say a word. I just obeyed. I looked for and found everything I needed to do.

The day that I recognized God, His mercy, and His grace that saved me, took me out of everything I was involved in, and gave me eternal life, my only prayer was, "Use me, use me, Lord!" And then, when He spoke to me and told me what I had to do to be used, I was speechless. In that silence, I understood how great His promises and His faithfulness were. I realized that I had to confront every situation, knowing that God was at my side and would not leave me.

We complicate things a lot and think that everything is hard to do, but when we have the will, it is there that God stretches out His precious hand and gives us a push, filling us with His strength to achieve it. When I realized that nothing was impossible for me, I finished my college studies with a degree in science and communications with a specialization in technology. A year after graduating, I began writing this book to share with you how he has guided me and transformed my life. If you depend on God completely, He will help you with what you need. You just have to have faith and trust that He will do it.

Believe me, it wasn't easy for me to write. I just had to yield and listen to His voice dictating to me word by word what needed to be in this book. The only thing I had to do was to face the situation, and God supported me with everything else.

Chapter 14
Let Us Not Become Stagnant

Don't get bogged down in the problem. Always think that there is a solution to every problem. Our state of mind may only allow us to see up to a certain point, but it doesn't mean that solving something is far from our reach or that there is simply no longer a solution. We are not alone. God's word says in Hebrews 13:5-6, "I will never desert you, nor will I ever forsake you so that we can confidently say 'The Lord is my helper;

14. Let Us Not Become Stagnant

I will not fear what man can do to me.'" Remember, if God is with us, nothing can stand against us.

I was very curious about the meaning of the word "mire." According to the dictionary, it means "a stretch of swampy or boggy ground." I also found another definition: "a situation or state of difficulty, distress, or embarrassment from which it is hard to extricate oneself." This word can basically be used to describe anything without the freedom to continue its course, being restrained by anything or anyone.

Many times throughout our life, we restrain our dreams and desires. That decision is made after experiencing difficult and ugly moments. We were mistreated, abused, or we felt pain affecting us to the point of failure. We lose all kinds of interest without knowing that at some point in life, in the future, we are going to say, "It's a shame I didn't do it!" It's interesting how our heart works. If we have a desire in our heart, this desire will remain there always inside. If we do what our heart desires, it will be done.

Whether the result is good or bad, it is better to try because if the result is bad, we can use that experience as a lesson to try something else the next time. That way, we will pay more attention and succeed in having a positive result. In many cases, we don't even try for fear of making a mistake or failing in it.

If we have the desire but never force ourselves to succeed in it, there will always remain in our hearts the desire and the curiosity of saying, "If I had only done it!" And we will stagnate. Imagine two wash basins. Only one is working properly. We turn on the faucet, and the water runs out and freely goes through the drain of the wash basin. The other one isn't working properly. It is stopped or blocked. After being in the wash basin for a while, the water will start to break down, decompose, and produce a foul odor that will increase until it contaminates the entire room.

I found these synonyms for the word stagnated:

1. Detained
2. Stopped
3. Suspended
4. Interrupted
5. Paralyzed
6. Bogged down
7. Immobilized

I also found the following synonyms for "to be decomposed":

1. To be messed up
2. To be put out of order
3. To be altered
4. To be disrupted
5. To be disturbed
6. To be stunned
7. To be disfigured
8. To be broken down

14. Let Us Not Become Stagnant

In general, we change our behavior with the bad circumstances and experiences of life. If we are really hurt, we automatically run back to our old defense mechanisms. We choose to be hermits. That means to be antisocial or to keep communicating with others but in a defensive way. We do that because we do not want to be hurt or to suffer as before. On the outside, we appear strong, yet we begin to act differently, look differently, and even have an illogical attitude. In other words, we try to conceal our real situation with a lie, "a breastplate or shield for our heart." We will note that people will not want to be around us, or we will opt to distance ourselves from others, enclose ourselves, and hold ourselves back on our walk.

Well then, we now know that we should not get bogged down with the problem. Therefore, we need to make a change to succeed in obtaining the solution. When we are determined to make a change, it is necessary to put some elements in place and to take out those that prevent the situation from being resolved.

Another example that we can see is moving from one place to another. Usually, we have two options. One option is to take along all our possessions and go through life with it all. The other is to look at our surroundings and decide what we are going to take, give away, or throw away because it is no longer of value. This is one form of organizing the "move." If we start to think about it and we choose the first option of taking everything, we may lose the chance to acquire new things, perhaps clothing or furniture. If we decide on the second option, besides a new home to remodel, we will have room for new things.

Another example that we can use is a vacuum cleaner.

Spritual Blindness

The job of a vacuum cleaner is to suck up waste, dust, etc. The vacuum cleaner has a bag whose function is to receive everything that is vacuumed from the place being cleaned. When this bag is clean and empty, it has all kinds of room to collect new elements. When the bag is full, logically, there isn't going to be room for anything. What's more, the vacuum cleaner won't be able to work the way it's supposed to. The motor will keep running, but when the bag gets filled and can't hold anymore, it will lose the ability to clean. We find ourselves with an overheated motor, a burning smell, an overfilled bag, and a vacuum cleaner too heavy to operate. Without you being offended, does this seem like a situation in your life? Is your life full of burdens? For what reason is it hard for your heart to function as it should?

I don't know if, at some time, you have experienced something like that of the vacuum cleaner, which I certainly have. One day, when I was alone in my church, I began to clean, and when it came time to vacuum the carpet, I plugged in the vacuum. When I turned it on, it was very heavy. I pushed it using all the strength I had. My back and my legs ached. I became irritated. The first thing that came into my mind was, "If I am working in my Father's house doing His will, why do I have to be in pain or irritated?" I began to question the goodness of God, but since God never abandons us, suddenly His voice came to my mind saying, "Empty the vacuum cleaner bag." I had been so preoccupied with the weight of the vacuum cleaner that I couldn't tell what the problem was.

When we are bogged down in a conflict, we don't think about the simplest things. The first thing we do is worry, then we get into a bad mood, and then we go crazy looking for a

14. Let Us Not Become Stagnant

solution. When I unzipped the vacuum to change the bag, not only was the bag full, but the dust was everywhere. Once I removed the bag, I had to clean the entire vacuum cleaner. It took me a long time to do it. When it was thoroughly clean, I started vacuuming again. As I pushed it, I applied the same pressure as I did when I had started to vacuum. It felt like it was self-propelled. My reaction made me laugh. I couldn't believe what had happened. I realized what God was showing me. And in the same way, I will show you even though you may get mad because of your situation. If you let Him guide you, he will show you the right way to act in each one of the difficult situations that you face in life.

Now, we have learned that we should not get bogged down in the situation we are in, and I refer to the spiritual, mental, or emotional one in your life. We can't dwell on the problem. Instead, we must look for a solution. Therefore, empty yourself by selecting and getting rid of your emotional, financial, and spiritual problems that disturb and bother you. Remove what is not useful to you. Give away what you no longer use. In other words, get rid of the things that bog you down.

It is very important to do it because, in this way, we make room for new things to come into our lives. You never know if new things will be better than the previous ones. The example of changing the vacuum cleaner shows us what our life is like in the material realm. It is the same in our personal and spiritual realms. I am referring to our personality, our soul, how we act toward others, how we treat ourselves, our character, the way we speak to others, how we react when others speak to us, and so on.

Spritual Blindness

The human being was created to subdue, to put into order, and to rule.

So then, when someone tells us what to do, we get offended, and we refuse to do it. But the truth is that if we allow ourselves to think and accept a correction or a suggestion from another person, it really shouldn't bother us. If we pay attention to the word "suggestion" it is basically an invitation to have the possibility or opportunity to change something for good. In this case, let us say that the evil of one situation can be changed into something good and thus can show others the right way.

Can you relate to any of the seven words in the first column of synonyms mentioned previously? Do you, perhaps, feel held back, paralyzed, or bogged down? If so, let us say this prayer together and out loud:

"Lord, now I see how my life has been held back, paralyzed, and even bogged down. I see that I cannot get out of this problem (say your problem aloud), and I need You to help me get out of it. I know in my heart that I have the authority and the power that You gave me when You went to the cross of Calvary for my sake. Therefore, I am saying this prayer in Your name, Jesus, to declare that today my situation is changing. In the name of Jesus, I cancel all the legal rights that Satan has had over me and in my life. I am no longer a slave, and therefore, nothing can hinder me, paralyze me, or bog me down. In the name of Jesus, I am going to begin a new and better path for my life. Lord, have Your will in me. Holy Spirit, free me, heal me, and restore me, in the name of Jesus. Amen."

14. Let Us Not Become Stagnant

"Come unto me all you who are burdened and heavy-laden, and I will give you rest." (Matthew 11:28)

Chapter 15
Like Trees

"Then God said, let the earth sprout vegetation, plants yielding seed and fruit trees on the earth bearing fruit after their kind with seed in them. And it was so. The earth brought forth vegetation, plants yielding seed after their kind and trees bearing fruit with seed in' their kind; and God saw that it was good." (Genesis 1: 11- 12)

15. Like Trees

In the life of a tree, there are different phases, periods, and changes. A maple tree experiences these changes according to its location and different climactic seasons.

Let us look at the four seasons: fall, winter, spring, and summer. If we pay attention to the change there is in a tree according to the season, we'll be able to appreciate what a real change is. These changes are quite evident because they are different from each other and go according to season. In the fall, the leaves change color; they turn from green to a clay-like color, to yellow, orange, or red, according to the tree. They start to fall from their branches one by one until the tree is bare. For a tree to complete its process, it has to let its leaves fall. Otherwise, in the next season, its shoots will not find any place to come out, and evidently, the leaves won't be able to be formed.

When nature gives way for winter to visit, the tree is already prepared to receive the cold temperature. At this time, the tree's structure is a dry, firm, robust trunk. Although we see it with a sad and lonely facade, it is in a moment of total absorption. It is working intensely to filter the best nutrients from the earth to begin a new stage.

If we pause to look in detail at a tree in winter, our perception will be: A dead-looking, dry, empty tree. Although we may see it as inactive, apparently without producing anything, it is actually in an active state, taking advantage of every nourishment that it finds under the soil.

In this way, its roots are nourished and strengthened for the time when spring and summer visit with much stronger heat. Then, it begins to offer its branches to the season, which become filled with shoots. Its sprouts are strengthened and are

Spritual Blindness

light green. The more sunlight the sprouts receive, the greener they become. The shoots are totally new; the sprouts have never known the previous leaves because when they arrived, the other leaves were no longer there. As the sun continues warming the earth, the sprouts grow, receiving from the trunk the nutrition that they need to become completely new and strong leaves.

With much satisfaction from having achieved its true identity or shape, the tree displays its colors, letting the summer know that it is ready for the new season.

When we moved to this new house, three things impressed me: the wood floors, the doors that divided the living- room from the dining room, and the two kitchen windows. Although I liked the wooden floors a lot, the kitchen windows were my pride and joy because the daylight entered through them while the sunset light reflected in my kitchen.

For many years, I loved to have breakfast in the morning, sitting at the kitchen table, contemplating the side yard of my house. Every morning, I would prepare my coffee with toast and fruit. While sitting in the chair eating, I would meditate on the sky, the trees, the birds, the squirrels, the planes, and the flowers. I could see everything from those two windows.

With time, I realized that God wanted to show me something that I looked at every morning but had never seen. It was the maple sugar tree in my neighbor's backyard. I had looked at it for many years but had never really seen it. This tree was four stories high, with a huge trunk and an immense crown. Anyone could see it.

In my case, I had looked at it, but I had never seen it. You can say that we overlook things in our daily lives without wanting to. We look, but we don't see – we hear, but we don't listen and lose many blessings because of it.

Up until now, in this chapter, we have seen what perfect photosynthesis is like, and it sounds amazing from the beginning to the end. However, other trees are not in the same condition. Some trees undergo storms and high winds from hurricanes. Some break, some are pulled out by the roots, and others are simply cut down. These trees have experienced strong impacts. Doesn't it look like us when we undergo defeat, pain, and suffering? We are left broken until we are empty, just like the wind breaks the branches of the trees until there are no branches anymore. We feel thirsty, down to the point of dying. God sees us every moment, waiting for us to come to Him so that He can restore us and heal our wounds.

When we feel weak, sad, and do not want to go on, it is then that Jesus becomes stronger to take us out of that state. Do you feel like a dry, old, and sad tree? He can transform you into the best tree. Jesus has the strength to harden your trunk and to fortify it. He has the power to do all new things. If this is your desire and need, He is the only one with the nutrients for your spirit, soul, and body.

I invite you to say this prayer out loud: Lord, today I recognize my weakness; I know that I am nothing without You. Today, I can hear your voice telling me, "Come, come to Me." Here I am, Lord, for You to take me, transform me. I am ready to let myself be transformed by You. Take my life, my heart, and my soul, and do your will with them. In the name of Jesus. Amen.

I have learned that the sugar maple tree is not only useful for displaying its beauty and producing sugar. It also provides shade and rest for animals. It keeps the forest healthy because it absorbs deep water and moistens different levels of the soil so that the top part of the ground is kept dry, and thus, it helps other plants and species. Its wood is considered one of the hardest and most expensive when used to make floors and furniture for the home.

There are different types of maples, but the sugar maple is the one that stands out the most. It has a very high production of maple syrup and is well recognized in Canada, which proudly displays the maple leaf on its flag.

Photosynthesis of the Maple Sugar Tree The maple sugar tree inhabits North America and was introduced in the year 1735. Its dimensions can be up to 82 feet high and as much as 49 feet wide. This tree grows best in full light. The type of soil where it grows is very light and fertile.

Photosynthesis begins when the tree starts to capture sugars at the end of the summer and the beginning of autumn. These sugars are changed into starch, and they stay in the roots for the winter. When winter visits this tree, the cold freezes the water, and the sap does not circulate. When spring comes, the starch that was accumulated in the roots for such a long time changes into sugar to balance its function enough to reactivate the tree's metabolism and, in this way, allow the tree to grow. When spring comes, the frozen or stored water (stored because of the cold temperature) begins to liquefy and circulate through the stem. The water is recognized as maple water. It is not sap. What we buy in the store is not what is taken directly from the

15. Like Trees

tree. This is an interesting process. To be able to extract the water, it is necessary to use adequate elements and to know how to do it. So, a person who doesn't know can make the tree sick, hurt it, and even kill it. Once the water is extracted from the trunk, it is collected in a container because it has to be boiled. Once it starts to boil and reaches the point of evaporation, the result is pure syrup, which we call "Maple Syrup."

The water that comes from the tree has a sour flavor. It must be processed to become what we buy as maple syrup in the supermarket, a real delicacy. Many people use this syrup as a natural sweetener in their coffee, tea, and other foods, like the famous American pancakes. It is one of the most expensive syrups, which is glass-bottled in a sophisticated form. To be able to extract this sugar water from a sugar maple tree, the tree must be no less than 40 years old. If you somehow identify with this process, tell the Lord, "Take the bitterness and the sourness from me and process me now so that I may be the sweetest for You with the best fragrance." "And God said, Behold, I have given you every seed-bearing plant that is on the surface of the earth and every tree that has fruit yielding seed; it shall be food for you." (Genesis 1:29)

Pray out loud: "Heavenly Father, You created me and gave me food to eat; my disobedience distanced me from You, and now this tree is weak, sad, and dry. Today, I recognize that without You, I can do nothing. Help me, Lord. Transform me into the prettiest tree possible. Give me Your wisdom, Your nourishment, Your strength. In Jesus' name. Amen."

Now, He will give you all the nourishment you need, but it is necessary to empty all the old stuff because, in this way, he can begin to give you everything you need, that is, His spiritual food. When you get this food, your shoots will begin to come out, and then you will have new leaves that will be strong and green, showing you the characteristics of a healthy, fresh, and pure tree.

Chapter 16
Trust Him

    "My son, do not forget my teaching, but let your heart keep my commandments; for the length of days and years of life they will add to you. Do not let kindness and truth leave you; bind them around your neck and write them on the tablet of your heart. So, you will find favor and good repute in the sight of God and man. Trust in the Lord with all your heart, and do not lean on your own understanding. In all your ways,

Spritual Blindness

acknowledge Him, and he will make your paths straight. Do not be wise in your own eyes; fear the Lord and turn away from evil. It will be healing to your body and refreshment to your bones. Honor the Lord from your wealth and from first of all, your produce so that your barns will be filled with plenty and your vats will overflow with new wine. My son, do not reject the discipline of the Lord or loathe His reproof. For whom the Lord loves, He reproves, even as a father corrects the son in whom he delights. How blessed is the man who finds wisdom and the man who gains understanding, for her profit is better than the profit of silver, and her gain better than fine gold. She is more precious than jewels, and nothing you desire compares with her. Long life is in her right hand; in her left hand are riches and honor. Her ways are pleasant ways, and all her paths are peace. She is a tree of life to all those who take hold of her, and happy are all who hold her fast. The Lord, by wisdom, founded the earth, by understanding, he established the heavens, by His knowledge, the deeps were broken up, and the skies dripped with dew. My son, let them not vanish from your sight; keep sound wisdom and discretion, so they will be life to your soul and adornment to your neck. Then, you shall walk in your way securely, and your foot will not stumble. When you lie down, you will not be afraid, when you lie down, your sleep will be sweet. Do not be afraid of sudden fear nor of the onslaught of the wicked when it comes, for the Lord will be your confidence and will keep your foot from being caught. Do not withhold good from those to whom it is due when it is in your power to do it. Do not say to your neighbor, 'go and come back, and tomorrow I will give it,' when you have it with you. Do not devise harm against your neighbor while he lives securely beside you. Do not contend with a man without cause, for he has done you no harm. Do not envy a man of violence, and do not choose any of his ways. For the devious are an abomination to the Lord, but He is intimate with the upright. The curse of the Lord is on the house of the wicked, but He blesses the dwelling of the righteous. Though He scoffs at the scoffers, yet He gives grace to the afflicted. The wise will inherit honor, but fools display dishonor." (Proverbs 3)

In the Bible, the proverbs are wise sayings of ethical teachings and of common sense about how to live a righteous life. I encourage you at this time to read the book of Proverbs so you can understand and have a deeper knowledge of God's plan for your life.

When our minds do not understand, it cannot analyze correctly. This is when we begin to test and trust other things. This distances us from God, and when we are distanced from Him, we also distance ourselves from His law. Not having His law, we don't have a guide to follow, and this makes us commit errors, and confusion begins to enter us. When you read Proverbs, read it slowly so you can understand them well. It's like when you are eating some delicacy; you savor that dish slowly and digest it very well.

Now, I am not comparing a proverb with a plate of food, but I want to ask you, when you read them, to appreciate and enjoy them to be able to feel satisfied. After understanding, you can value life and learn to see it from another perspective; you will be able to perceive God's message, and you will learn to walk with Him.

People who walk without God confuse things. They lose everything moral and ethical.

They confuse liberty with depravity, and their behavior is not pleasing to God. Justifying themselves, they say, "But what happens is that You don't understand, Lord, I trust You!" But the Lord says, "You say that you trust me, but in reality, you are not surrendering your problem to me!" How can you stop worrying about something you keep on carrying? Suddenly, you are asking yourself, "How should I do it? How do I resolve this?" Or you say, "I want to get out of this," or "I want to straighten myself up, but I can't." And it is very common to think that way, especially when we do things in our own strength or in our own way. It is because we don't know God, and we have never had a conversation or a relationship with Him, and we fail.

You may say to me, "Well, I have been a Christian for many years... I'm from such and such a denomination. I am a son/daughter of pastors. I am the second or fifth generation of really well-known pastors." I am not referring to denominations or generations, but when

Jesus returns, He won't be looking for titles, denominations, or the most well-decorated churches. He is coming to look for our souls, and it is for this reason that God requires your heart now. It is of the utmost importance to guard our hearts because we can all be Christians, but the real question is: "Do you have a personal relationship with Jesus? Is He your first love? (Revelation 2:4) Are you willing to wait on Him? (Psalm 40:1) Is He your Daddy?" (Galatians 3:26) Can you, perhaps, identify Jesus as something like this in your life? Nothing or no one can compare with Jesus; only He has the power to change everything for the good. This is called salvation.

16. Trust Him

It is of utmost importance to have a close relationship with Him. Enough of religion, enough of competing, enough of fighting among believers. We should start sharing with others the meaning of being a follower of Christ. How is this to be done? Ask God what He wants you to be like. Build a relationship with Him. He will show you the way to act, step by step. Perhaps you don't have the answers to these questions because of the simple fact that you don't know what it is to have or feel love, and I am referring to real love. What's more, you have never experienced the love that I am referring to: the first love of Jesus. Have you asked yourself, "What is she talking to me about?" It's the same when I mention if He is your best friend because you have or have had a best friend, and at some time, he or she has failed you, and it's hard for you to trust them again. And you realize that you have never had a best friend. And it's the same when I mention if you consider God as "Your Daddy." Maybe you don't know what it is to have a father. In fact, the one that you may see as your father, the one who provides food and clothing or the one who takes care of you, has never had the ability to fill the void inside of you and has not known how to love you with the love of the father that you need. Or he himself, the one whom you trusted as a father, and you felt protected, suddenly took advantage of you and physically molested you. Then, when someone talks about God being a "Daddy", the only thing you can see is a masculine image that you distance yourself from because you think He would do the same; or you simply don't want or can't trust Him through all the pain you have been carrying during this time.

At this time, your memory is working at a rapid pace, bringing to it remembrances of your past, and I say to you, "Glory to God for that!" Don't feel bad; this is actually good because God is bringing to light all these things so that you can cancel everything that happened long ago. This is your time to cancel, in Jesus' name, every past negative thing and every generational curse. This is the time for forgiving the people who have offended you and for forgiving yourself.

When you forgive others and forgive yourself, you release blessings in your life. At some time in your life, you have thought with respect to what they did to you that it had been your fault. It is important that you are very sure that what happened to you was not your fault. That thought has come directly from the devil with the purpose of preventing you from becoming free. The devil wants to keep you tied to your past so you will continue to be unhappy, depressed, sick, and so on.

Do you know why mistreated and offended people think it was their fault? It is simply because they feel dirty inside and think that God has disqualified them from being at His side. The devil takes advantage of this and makes them think it was only the fault of the affected one in order to paralyze them so that they can't speak or defend themselves. Or they can't get out of this mental prison because he imposes fear on them, and that fear paralyzes that person. But God gives us a spirit of power, love, and self-control. (2 Timothy 1:7)

Rise up as you are, child of God! He has never abandoned you- the devil made you think so, and it is a lie. God never forgets us. Rise up and say to the devil, "Enough! Your party with me is over. I am no longer your victim! I don't believe you anymore, you liar!"

Declare out loud:

16. Trust Him

"God, you are my heavenly Father, Jesus, you are my first love. You are my best friend, and I trust you. I declare this on earth as it is in heaven, in the name of Jesus. Amen."

To trust God is to rest in Him, and to believe Him is to have the victory. "Commit your way to God, trust also in Him, and he will do it." (Psalm 37:5)

I remember when I met Christ, it was very hard to trust Him because I had been very hurt in my past, especially by men. When I was just a little girl, my parents gave me permission to have my first boyfriend. I trusted him because our parents were friends. My parents never found out what this young man did to me. I never told anyone about my abuse. First, I became afraid of him because every time he abused me, I was speechless and immobilized. Second, I never wanted to say anything because I needed to protect my father. If my father had found out how this young man abused me, he would have made a very wrong decision. At the time of this abuse, I was an immature little girl and in a position in which I did not care about protecting myself but about protecting my father. I did not want to see my father in jail, especially for defending me. I made the decision to defend my father and, at the same time, continued to be a victim of abuse.

I saw a case like what happened to me a few years ago when my oldest son asked me if I had heard about his best (girl) friend. I met this little girl when she was just two years old, and she and my son used to play together in my house. She was a little doll with her curly hair. Then, they grew up and continued to be friends. Sadly, at nineteen years of age, her ex-boyfriend abused her until he took her life. When I saw this picture, my own past came to my mind, and it is now that I can see the

Spritual Blindness

mercy and glory of God in my life for having protected me. And I asked the Lord, "Why, my God, does this happen? Why, when a person attacks another person, do they become immobile and can't defend themselves?"

There are cases in which the man is stronger than the woman, but there are also cases in which the woman is stronger than the man. I am referring to the physical, but when someone is attacked, they cannot respond to defend themselves. When we are not covered with the blood of Christ, Satan knows it. When we are attacked, groped, abused, or raped, it's because of being uncovered from God's protection. Satan takes advantage of us to paralyze us so we can't move. Although we want to defend ourselves, there is something stronger that will not let us do anything, both physically and verbally.

Before I met Christ, my father was my best friend. We had a beautiful relationship. I was always attached to him, and I liked to share a lot with him. And this was not only when I was a little girl, but even when I was eighteen years old, we often went bicycle riding holding hands. We were a family of four daughters, and my father was totally against physical abuse. My father never put his hand on us, and he didn't agree with my mother when she wanted to discipline us with a spanking. My father's discipline was a very strict one based on communication. He would explain things to us, the good and the bad, and when we understood that what we had done was bad, he would correct us with a punishment, such as not going out of the house for a certain amount of time or doing household chores.

Going back to the situation with my boyfriend, I thought I had to be quiet and keep enduring everything he did to me to

16. Trust Him

protect my father and because I didn't have the courage to leave him. Once, I told him we needed to stop our relationship because it was unhealthy for me and for him. He got so mad that he pushed me in such a way that I fell to the ground and hit my head on the cement. He could have killed me. I became even more afraid of him, and I decided to continue the relationship, although he made me do what he did. My boyfriend then threatened me and told me that if I left him, there was no telling what he would do.

What a pity that my fear and my lack of experience didn't let me go to the authorities to tell them about him. But if God allowed it, it was because He had another plan. Anyway, when he got tired of doing everything he wanted to with me, he was the one who left me. And for me, it was a breath and relief. Although I was already used to being mistreated and abused, in my future relationships, I felt a little confused when I would meet nice young men. I couldn't appreciate the good treatment because I was used to something totally different, that is, abuse. The abuse was a behavior that I had learned from a previous relationship and had become a "normal" thing.

After all my experiences with my first boyfriend, I realized many things, one of which was not to trust others. When these young men would tell me nice things, I would think they were lying to me, simply saying nice things so that I would give in and they could do the same thing as before, so they could hurt me. Then, so as not to be hurt, I covered myself with a strong shield. In this way, I was the one in control of my relationships, manipulating the situation in my own way. By using the physical beauty of a woman to conquer the heart, my sole purpose was to hurt because I had been hurt. The pain was what I had received, and therefore, it was the only thing I could give.

I know I wasn't the only child or woman abused on this earth, and it is because of this that God placed me here to write all these truths so you can understand your situation. He isn't taking notes about how many people you have hurt or how many people have hurt you. He is telling you that He wants to heal your heart as He did mine years ago. He is the only one who can change a person. Trust Him and suffer no more.

Suffering is not from God- it is from Satan. Satan wants us to have suffering, to be unhappy, despised, groped, attacked, raped. We were not created for this. We were created to be loved and to be able to love.

The question is," Are you afraid to love or to trust?" And if the answer is "Yes," the reason is that when you believed you were loved or not loved, you were defeated. What you thought was love was a falsification compared to real love. Solution: Invite God into your heart, and He will show you real love. Only He has real love because He first loved us so that we could know that love and be able to love others. God is love. (1 John 4:7- 11) For you to love, you really must know what love is. You can't give something that you don't have and, in fact, you do not have.

Let us pray, "Heavenly Father, today I want to receive Your love. Forgive me for looking for love in the wrong place. I ask You to forgive me. I take from Satan the legal right that he took in my life by making me think it was impossible to believe in You. Now, in Jesus' name, I declare myself free, and I receive Your love, Lord. Amen."

Chapter 17
The Power of God While We Wait

"Who do you say that I am?" (Matthew 16:15) In other words, "How great do you think my power is? How much do you think I can do, change, adjust, raise, lower, smooth out, or straighten out?"

"Now when Jesus came into the district of Caesarea Philippi, He was asking His disciples, 'Who do people say that the

Son of Man is?' And they said, 'Some say John the Baptist, and others, Elijah; but still others, Jeremiah, or one of the prophets.' He said to them, 'But who do you say that I am?' Simon Peter answered, 'You are the Christ, the Son of the living God.' And Jesus said to him, 'Blessed are you, Simon Bar-Jonah! Because flesh and blood did not reveal this to you, but My Father who is in heaven. I also say to you that you are Peter, and upon this rock, I will build My church, and the gates of Hades will not overpower it. I will give you the keys of the kingdom of heaven, and whatever you bind on earth shall have been bound in heaven, and whatever you loose on earth shall have been loosed in heaven." (Matthew 16:13-19)

In this passage, we realize the power that our Heavenly Father has. When Jesus asked Peter who he said He was, Jesus already knew the answer because He knew what Peter would say. Let us note how great God's mercy is because when Peter answered Jesus, who he thought He was, He not only blessed him because of the Father's revelation, but He also changed his name from Simon to Peter.

Why did Jesus change his name? This was a necessary illustration that to be able to understand once we accept Him, invite Him into our hearts, and believe in Him, He changes us from the inside out. We come weak to His feet to receive His strength, and then, as strong people, we will be able to go forward. If your heart's desire is to change, Jesus can help you. He will do it from the inside out. Only He can change the life of a person. You will stop being what you used to be, and you will do things God's way. The Lord says that He knows us from our mother's womb. "Before I formed you in the womb, I knew

17. The Power of God While We Wait

you, and before you were born, I consecrated you." (Jeremiah 1:5)

He knows our thoughts, and He even knows how many hairs we have on our heads.

Unfortunately, through man's disobedience, we were transformed to that which is of the world. We live a life separated from God, using pretexts to justify what we do.

Couples that are about to get married often make the decision to live together first. This way, they can save money for an expensive wedding. They do not realize they are fornicating. Others have children while single, some change their sex, and thousands of wrong pretexts that only serve to satisfy their rebellion or their own desires, without knowing that those decisions take them to a spiritual death because they are doing things out of the order of God, our Creator.

It costs us to wait on God because we are not aware of His power. We think that we are the ones who have the power, and we decide to do things our way. That is called rebellion and lack of knowledge because we ignore what the Bible tells us. When we know what God's power is, we simply want to trust Him and believe in Him. No longer do we just decide for ourselves, but rather, He decides in us, and that way, we see His power. When we decide to wait on His power and follow Him, our lives will be less complicated. Let Him transform your life and so become what He created for you in the beginning.

It's interesting to see when Jesus asked Peter in particular who he said He was because, at the time of His crucifixion, Je-

Spritual Blindness

sus knew Peter would deny Him three times. But it was necessary to change his name to give him identification and strength since Peter's name means "stone" (something hard and stable), and Simon means "reed" (something that is soft and can bend).

You are going to see moments in your lives where, in one way or another, you will deny Jesus. Perhaps in times of sadness, loneliness, depression, or sickness, when you don't even have the strength to talk, you are flat on your back, and anxiety enters your mind, and you think you're going crazy and you are not finding a way out, and you may even think you're going to die. It is then when you must seek His face, seek Him with your whole being and strength, and you must reach out your hand to take Jesus', and have the assurance that He is faithful.

A problem occurs because it is hard for us to wait. We want everything right now. While we are waiting, we don't realize that God is touching us, building us up, or moulding us. Let us get to know God and His power. We concentrate so much on what we want, and we ask Him for things when all the while He is saying to us, "I want you to get to know me first, I want you to understand my ways and rules, and then when you have that understanding, I will be able to give you what you are asking me for. What use is it for God to give you what you are asking for before you know what to do with it? It is better to get to know Him first so that when He grants us the desire of our hearts, we will have the ability to know how to use it. It is more important to know how to use what He gives us and to have the assurance that He will receive the glory.

Do not complain anymore; just trust in His power and have the certainty that He will do it.

17. The Power of God While We Wait

"For from Him and through Him and to Him are all things. To Him be the glory forever.

Amen." (Romans 11:36) "So let no one boast in men. For all things belong to You, whether Paul or Apollos or Cephas or the world or life or death or things present or things to come; all things belong to you, and you belong to Christ, and Christ belongs to God." (1 Corinthians 3:21-23)

Let us not doubt God because if we doubt, it is because we do not trust. If we do not trust, we deny Him, and we make Him null and void. And if we make Him null and void and we deny Him, who takes God's place in our lives? If you want God to change your life for good now, just talk to Him and tell Him that. He has been waiting for you for a long time. Don't think about it anymore, don't doubt anymore, and trust in Him.

Open your heart, your mouth, your mind; speak with sincere words; call out to Him, "Father, I need you!" Recognize and repent of every sin you have committed that is separating you from Him. Remember that the devil brings thoughts (darts) to keep you separated from God and His good purpose in your life.

When we confess our sins, He forgives us. Do not forget that at the end of human life, there is eternal life and that if you decide for Jesus now, you will have salvation here today. You will have freedom in your soul and a spirit to live life according to the plans and purposes of the Father. And when your life is over, you will be sure to enter eternity with Jesus Christ because He only is the way, the truth, and the life. (John 14:6) Keep your hope in God, and you will see His power. I assure you that if you believe, you will see the glory of God in your life. By keeping your hopes in Him and waiting on Him, you will receive the needed strength to discover God's purpose for your life, even if you have no idea what that is.

The plan and purpose that God had for Abraham and Sarah was to be fulfilled in God's time. The only thing they had to do was to wait for God's time in their lives. This is to trust fully in God's promise. God told Abraham to count the stars and that His blessings would be more than they were.

He spoke to him about the nations that would follow him, including sons and daughters. Sarah couldn't grasp God's power in her life, what God could do, the changes He would make in her. I imagine that because she was present at so many births, helping women, the desire to have a son was turning into a failure, bringing frustration to her life, listening to those voices saying words like, "Look how God loves you and He hasn't given you a son" or " and you keep on believing"... the voices of envy and jealousy would speak to her unceasingly..." your husband will leave you for another who will give him sons..." and thousands of other words that would torture Sarah's mind to the point of selling her soul to the devil.

Sarah didn't let God accomplish His plan for her life in His time, and for that, she had to pay many consequences. It brought a lot of pain into her life and that of others because she took control of the whole situation. She took control when she gave Abraham her maid to go to bed with him. In this way, she would finally have a son. In her great desperation, she did not realize that she would never be the mother of that creature.

When we go ahead of God's plan, we make mistakes. She sinned by not believing in God's power. She was complicit in the adultery and fornication that her husband and maid committed. This desperation brought consequences to their lives, and they had to wait many years for her to finally conceive a son. It is very important to wait on God for you to be able to see His power. I call it "God's power while we wait "because for me to be able to see His glory manifested in my life, I had to learn to wait on Him.

Chapter 18
Dominion Over Everything

"Then God said, 'Let us make man in Our image, according to Our likeness; and let them have dominion over the fish of the sea, and over the birds of the sky, and over the cattle, and over all the earth, and over every creeping thing that creeps on the earth.'" (Genesis 1:26) The word dominion refers to the authority or command that one has over something. It also refers to having a rule over something.

18. Dominion Over Everything

If we were created with this desire of God, it means that we can speak to our problems, ordering them to submit, whether it be impossible situations or bodily sicknesses. Our authority will make every circumstance work in our favor. We were created in His image and likeness for lordship over everything, even animals that "creep." The serpent, as well as the other animals, were created to obey. Unfortunately, Eve was deceived by the serpent because she did not know the power that God gave her.

When we understand our potential in Christ and apply it, we will realize that all things must be submitted under our feet. God created everything in six days, placing it at our service, being assured that we would lack nothing, thus being able to serve Him without any excuse, doing His will.

This tells me that when we walk with God, we won't lack anything. He created it all before forming us. Therefore, it is done and made available for us and for no one else, not even for the rest of creation. Everything is available for every person who lives for God.

When we come to understand this, we will realize that those who keep following Jesus do not have to be experiencing any need, whether it be economic, physical, emotional, etc.

Misery cannot exist in us or in our family because we are sons and daughters of a powerful King who is the owner of all. If you have some economic need, start to claim it and order the devil to return all your belongings because they are yours. It is the inheritance that God gave you.

Spritual Blindness

Now repeat this aloud: "In the name of Jesus, Satan, give me back everything you have taken from me. It is my inheritance. Before, I wasn't aware of the power Jesus had given me, but today, I know that power because He lives in me, and I order you to release the inheritance that God left to me. It is mine. Release it in the name of Jesus right now. Amen."

When we were little children, we had needs. We would run to our earthly father for his help. Our fathers did whatever was possible to help us. How much more will our Heavenly Father do to help us. He delights when we come into His presence. I remember when I was jumping on top of my father, giving him many kisses and hugs, and touching him lovingly, I could see his face full of joy. Our Heavenly Father reacts in the same way when we come up to Him, demanding a hug, a smile, and His help.

It's not easy to trust someone after having had an unpleasant experience in life. At the same time, we cannot keep going on tolerating pain, hurting others, or continue to be victims of suffering. In the book of Genesis, the Bible says that God created everything and saw that it was all good. God said human beings were very good. Then, the evil one came and changed it all. We were created to be good and to do good, but we were deceived, mistreated, and we became evil. Glory to God for His mercy and grace when He sent His son Jesus to pay for our suffering and sin. He chose to suffer so that today, you and I might be free of all suffering, pain, physical and mental abuse. At the same time, let us stop hurting others.

All the suffering that I dragged through the years was because the devil held me in bondage and deceit. He did not let me speak because when you speak, you are set free. The truth

18. Dominion Over Everything

makes us free. As I kept silent, I continued experiencing mistreatment, and I was overwhelmed by the matter. I met more young men and had many boyfriends. The consequences led to emotional and spiritual death. Incidentally, that was the devil's plan for my life, but not my Father God's plan.

The reason I felt this way was because the sin I was carrying produced spiritual death. Jesus came to give us life by removing sin with His power. He did not come to give us a religion; man formed that. Let me tell you that religion distances you from Jesus. An intimate relationship with Jesus is the best thing that can happen to you. Because He is authentic and original, He will show you what is true and not the imitations of things. Jesus is real. Something very important that we must know is God alone is the Creator.

In the beginning, God created Lucifer, who later on, because of pride, became the devil! God is divine, holy, glorious, good, powerful, merciful, full of grace, majestic, and the King of kings. He is the Great I Am, the Alpha and Omega, the Beginning and the End, and more. The devil is not original. He is a copier, a falsifier. He copies what God did and does. The devil is not authentic. His identity is wicked, destroyer, manipulator, liar, egotist, false, and more.

The entire sacrifice that Jesus made on the cross was to destroy the works of the devil. Religion separates us from the presence of Jesus. How many times have you tried to go to a church and felt dirty? In your mind, you saw other people looking at you as a tremendous sinner. How many times have you said you weren't going to attend again because you didn't agree with what the priest or the pastor was saying? You wouldn't place an offering in the basket because you didn't

Spritual Blindness

know what they were doing with the money. All that is religion. Let's not look at what others are doing. This is a distraction of the devil. He wants you to concentrate on what is around you so you can't see what God has for you. Let us place our attention on what God wants us to do. Focus clearly on the Heavenly Father. Remember that we have dominion, lordship, authority, and power over everything, even over the demons that are around here. "Your kingdom is an everlasting kingdom, and your dominion endures throughout all generations." (Psalm 145:13). "How great are His signs and how mighty are His wonders! His kingdom is an everlasting kingdom, and His dominion is from generation to generation." (Daniel 4:3)

It is important that on this day, you begin to renounce the consequences of former generations. You don't inherit anything from them because the inheritance that they had was not God's inheritance for you. Renounce your generational inheritances. Take your place in Christ. Tell the devil, "No more!" Start to walk with your King, the one who formed you from your mother's womb. Draw near to Him, believe in Him. He loves you.

And He said, "Before I formed you, I knew you in the womb, and before you were born, I consecrated you..." (Jeremiah 1:5)

"Yours, O LORD, is the greatness and the power, and the glory and the victory and the majesty, indeed everything that is in the heavens and the earth; Yours is the dominion, O LORD, and You exalt Yourself as head over all. Both riches and honor come from You, and You rule over all, and in Your hand is power and might; and it lies in Your hand to make great and to strengthen everyone. Now, therefore, our God, we thank

You and praise Your glorious name. But who am I, and who are my people that we should be able to offer as generously as this? For all things come from You and from Your hand, we have given You.

For we are sojourners before You, and tenants, as all our fathers were; our days on the earth are like a shadow that does not last. O LORD our God, all this abundance that we have provided to build You a house for Your holy name, it is from Your hand, and all is Yours. Since I know, O my God, that You try the heart and delight in uprightness, I, in the integrity of my heart, have willingly offered all these things; so now with joy I have seen Your people, who are present here, make these offerings willingly to You. O LORD, the God of Abraham, Isaac and Israel, our fathers, preserve this forever in the intentions of the heart of Your people, and direct their heart To You." (1 Chronicles 29:11-18)

Direct your heart to Jesus Christ, to the Father, and the power of the Holy Spirit will never disappoint you. Your eyes will be open and will see the truths of God.

"The Lord opens the eyes of the blind; The Lord raises up those who are bowed down; the Lord loves the righteous." (Psalm 146:8)

References

These references were used for the Spanish Edition Book and has been translated into English.

Dictionary of the Royal Spanish Academy from: http:/www.rae.es

J. Strong. New Strong's Comprehensive Concordance of the Bible, 2002."

The Holy Bible. New American Standard 1960 (NAS)

W E. Vine, Vine's Exhaustive Expository Dictionary of Old and New Testament Words, 2003.

Made in the USA
Middletown, DE
10 November 2024

64240702R00086